Implementing Quality Improvement and Change in the Early Years

Education at SAGE

SAGE is a leading international publisher of journals, books, and electronic media for academic, educational, and professional markets.

Our education publishing includes:

- accessible and comprehensive texts for aspiring education professionals and practitioners looking to further their careers through continuing professional development

- inspirational advice and guidance for the classroom

- authoritative state of the art reference from the leading authors in the field

Find out more at: **www.sagepub.co.uk/education**

Implementing Quality Improvement and Change in the Early Years

Edited by
Michael Reed and Natalie Canning

⑤SAGE

Los Angeles | London | New Delhi
Singapore | Washington DC

First published 2012

SAGE Publications Ltd
1 Oliver's Yard
55 City Road
London EC1Y 1SP

SAGE Publications Inc.
2455 Teller Road
Thousand Oaks, California 91320

SAGE Publications India Pvt Ltd
B 1/I 1 Mohan Cooperative Industrial Area
Mathura Road
New Delhi 110 044

SAGE Publications Asia-Pacific Pte Ltd
33 Pekin Street #02-01
Far East Square
Singapore 048763

Library of Congress Control Number: 2011921968

British Library Cataloguing in Publication data
A catalogue record for this book is available from the British Library

ISBN 978-0-85702-168-7
ISBN 978-0-85702-169-4 (pbk)

Typeset by Kestrel Data, Exeter, Devon
Printed in India by Replika Press Pvt Ltd
Printed on paper from sustainable resources

This book is for
Clare, Rachel, Joshua, Jacob, Molly, Olivia Grace,
Pujaah, Simaren, Tess, Oliver, Christopher, Sian, Cassie,
Caoimhe, Faolan, Phoebe, Dan, Jake, Jesse
and children everywhere

Contents

List of tables and figures

Acknowledgements

This book would not have been possible without the valuable contributions from individuals and groups who have taken part in research and been critical readers for chapters. In particular we would like to thank all the inspirational Early Years Professionals and the students from the BA and Foundation Degree in Early Years at the University of Worcester who have helped shape the views expressed in various chapters through their stimulating discussion and reflection on practice.

We also thank colleagues from local authorities and members of the Birmingham Early Years and Childcare Team, partner agencies and childcare providers for their expertise and advice, and Professor Etienne Wenger who allowed his workshop materials to be shared. Particular thanks go to Karen Hanson for her support and Karen Campbell, Jo McLellan, Sue Podmore and Elaine Redding for help with critical reading. Finally, we would like to thank Alex Molineux and Jude Bowen at Sage for their advice and support.

About the editors and contributors

Editors

Michael Reed is a Senior Lecturer at the Centre for Early Childhood, within the Institute of Education at the University of Worcester. He teaches on undergraduate and postgraduate courses and shares a coordinating role for a large Foundation Degree programme in early years which is taught in partner colleges and at children's centres within the community. He has been part of course development and writing teams at the Open University and is an experienced author. He co-edited *Reflective Practice in the Early Years* (2010) and most recently *Work-Based Research in the Early Years* (2011), both published by Sage.

Natalie Canning is a lecturer in Education – Early Years at the Open University. Her background is in playwork and social work, particularly supporting children to explore personal, social and emotional issues through play. She has published a number of articles relating to professional development and the early years and has presented at national and European conferences. Her main research is in the areas of children's empowerment in play and she is currently involved in research on developing children as autonomous learners. She has taught across a variety of early childhood undergraduate and postgraduate programmes and has edited *Play and Practice in the Early Years Foundation Stage* (2011) and co-edited *Reflective Practice in the Early Years* (2010), both published by Sage.

Contributors

Mandy Andrews is a Senior Lecturer at the University of Worcester in the Centre for Early Childhood within the Institute of Education. She teaches on Early Years Professional Status pathways and under- graduate and postgraduate modules in early childhood. She was formerly Project Director of a large Sure Start Local Programme and Children's Centre in Cornwall. Her research interests include leadership and children's play and empowerment.

Karen Appleby is a Senior Lecturer in Early Childhood and Learning and Teaching Fellow at the University of Worcester. She is Partnership Coordinator for the Centre for Early Childhood, in the Institute of Education, and teaches across a variety of early childhood programmes. Previously she has worked as the Course Leader for the BA (Hons) Integrated Early Childhood Studies and HND in Early Childhood Studies.

Sue Baylis is a Senior Lecturer and Course Leader for the Early Years Professional Status programme within the Centre for Early Child- hood, at the University of Worcester. She has extensive experience within the early years sector. Prior to working at the University of Worcester she was employed at a nursery assessment unit attached to a special school that catered for children with moderate to severe learning difficulties. Her main research is in areas of empowering children with special educational needs to have a 'voice'. She has taught across a range of early childhood undergraduate and postgraduate programmes and co-authored a chapter in *Reflective Practice in the Early Years* (2010), published by Sage.

Rory McDowall Clark originally trained as a nursery and primary teacher. She has had a wide range of experience in broader social contexts including community development with charities and voluntary organisations and outreach youth work. Rory worked as an educational consultant for a number of local authorities before taking up a post in the Centre for Early Childhood at the University of Worcester where she has been a Senior Lecturer for the past ten years. Her research interests include gender, cultural views of the child and continuing professional development. She is the author of *Childhood in Society for Early Childhood Studies* (2010), published by Learning Matters.

Alison Murphy is a Senior Early Years Consultant for a rural local au- thority supporting quality improvement for early years care and educa- tion including childminding settings and children's centres. Alison has a background in early years teaching both in the UK and overseas, run- ning a rural voluntary pre-school setting, in the regulation of daycare settings and more recently in supporting settings and children's centres to develop quality improvement through graduate leadership and con- tinuous professional development.

Sue Owen is Director of the Well-being Department at the National Children's Bureau (NCB) in London and before that was Director of NCB's Early Childhood Unit. Previously she was Deputy Director of the Early Years National Training Organisation and lead officer for early years at Humberside County Council. She has also worked as Information Officer for the National Childminding Association, as Playgroup Adviser for Manchester City Council, Childminding Adviser for the Save the Children Fund and as a freelance researcher. Sue's most recent publication, with Steph Petrie, is *Authentic Relationships in Group Care for Infants and Toddlers* (Jessica Kingsley, 2006), and her doctorate was on the development of organised systems of childminding. Sue is also currently

Early Years Theme Lead for the Centre for Excellence and Outcomes in Children's and Young People's Services (C4EO).

Claire Majella Richards is Senior Lecturer and Course Leader for the Integrated Early Childhood Studies Degree within the Institute of Education at the University of Worcester. She has extensive experience of multi-agency partnership working, having been employed within the voluntary and statutory sectors. Her roles have been varied, in the fields of mental health nursing, substance misuse services, and lately with the social concern of domestic abuse. As a qualified barrister, she remains a committed advocate to the rights of children and is engaged with the activities of the local Safeguarding Children Board.

Parm Sansoyer is a freelance Early Years Inspector with extensive experience in inspecting the full range of early years provision. She has worked directly with families and children in various contexts and as a therapist dealing with domestic violence, sexual abuse and mental health issues. This brings her into contact with a range of other professional disciplines. She has recently been part of a team exploring communities of practice led by colleagues from the Open University. She holds a BA honours degree in Early Childhood Studies and has particular interests in equality, diversity and inclusion.

Carla Solvason is a Senior Lecturer in the Centre for Early Childhood within the Institute of Education at the University of Worcester. Part of her role involves working closely with eight partner colleges that deliver the University's Foundation Degree in Early Years. Prior to lecturing Carla worked as a researcher, a consultant for schools looking to create communication-rich environments, and a primary school teacher. She has published work relating to school culture, educational equality and social justice, collaborative working and work-based research.

Linda Tyler is a Senior Lecturer at the University of Worcester in the Centre for Early Childhood. Previously she has worked as a teacher and coordinator for ICT, Literacy and Science in a Becta award-winning school. She has designed and delivered ICT training for a local authority and developed several ICTogether groups to enhance parent ICT skills working with parents and children. She is researching the effects of podcasting on children's communication skills in order to develop a teacher training package for students. She has published work online about the use of avatars as a medium for improving literacy.

Rosie Walker is a social worker by training who has worked in a variety of childcare settings, including social care, child guidance, NSPCC and child protection training. She has acted as a Guardian ad Litem and set up a Family Support Service as well as being an Associate Tutor on the NPQICL course for two years. For the last seven years she has managed two phase 1 children's centres and in 2010 joined the University of Worcester as a Senior Lecturer in the Centre for Early Childhood.

Introduction

Michael Reed and Natalie Canning

The central argument to this book is that quality improvement is part of an evolving and changing process of ideas, innovations and implementations. As such the process of quality improvement has seen early childhood education and practice move towards an integrated child-focused service. We have both observed this shift when working closely with practitioners involved in implementing change. We have shared their despair when having to enact yet another development driven by a myriad government directives, their elation when gaining a qualification or their successes in working with families as part of integrated community support. We recognise the dedication of practitioners and the goodwill they give freely in order to improve quality experiences for children and families. We also recognise that there are now practitioners who have been in post for a decade or more who know that change is one of the few certainties in their professional lives. It is these practitioners who are making change happen, turning rhetoric into reality and making a positive difference for children's life experiences. Consequently we are now embedding into practice integrated working with other agencies, acknowledging the significance of parental partnerships and building on holistic development through a play-based curriculum.

Early years, perhaps more than any other profession in the last decade, has been concerned with improving quality practice through evaluation and reflection, resulting in opportunities to study for qualifications or undertake training. Practitioners are embracing initiatives for improving quality and tackling strategies to implement change head on. This has resulted in new ways of thinking and doing things and change in local and national policies throughout the UK. These new initiatives have placed competing demands on practitioners and early years settings and require not only implementation but an ongoing review and evaluation of practice. The list below demonstrates just some of the demanding directives that have emerged from changes in early years policy:

- regulatory or inspection frameworks, which demand a detailed review of practice and policies to support practice;

- integrated or partnership working evaluated as part of the inspection process;

- guidance and coordinated strategies, which ask practitioners to work together in order to protect vulnerable children, for example the common assessment framework (CAF);

- workforce development organisations, which set out professional expectations placed upon practitioners;

- quality improvement frameworks, both nationally and locally;

- curriculum policies, plans and directives, which include ways to educate children, promote a play-based curriculum, develop creativity and protect children;

- training and qualifications that require review of policies, integrated working and active collaboration with parents;

- parental partnerships, which are now an integrated part of curriculum planning and policy review for settings and children's centres.

All these place high levels of expectation upon practitioners, which are well intentioned and have the welfare of children at heart but sometimes give a 'mechanistic' view of early years practice. Importance is placed on setting targets, achieving professional expectations and meeting regulations, which are all seen as marks of quality. In itself these indicators are not prohibitive in terms of improving quality, but raise certain questions, such as, who decides what quality looks like? Importantly, does having quality laid out as a sometimes static view of practice inhibit innovation, because practitioners might then only aspire to a 'set level' of quality? In addition, there are inspection frameworks that tend to give an external view of quality rather than encourage those who lead practice to decide for themselves how to review and implement policy. Perhaps this tells us that we should consider quality in terms of *how* practice is evaluated and see this as just as important as *what* is evaluated.

These issues are explored in Section 1 of the book, which questions quality as a product or process. In the first chapter Michael Reed considers how quality is defined and what this looks like in practice. He exposes some of the tensions that exist between regulation and locally determined views about quality and summarises the enormous range of literature surrounding what we call 'quality practice'. The theme continues into Chapter 2, where he and Sue Owen focus on childminding as an essential and highly important part of quality early years provision. They expose tensions between regulators and government that sometimes fail to recognise the unique aspects of a childminder's role. They also highlight the benefits of practitioners working together as part of a network to share and respond to new ideas and change. The central theme of working together within a quality process is explored in Chapter 3 where Michael Reed and Parm Sansoyer consider integrated working and its value to promoting quality. They argue that there is a need to consider how we all operate within a landscape of practice that means adhering to different ways of seeing and doing things. This requires a view of practice that requires reflection on practice, or more appropriately, developing reflective practice. The last chapter in this section argues that quality processes cannot exist without reflective practice, and Karen Appleby and Mandy Andrews expose the interrelationship between values, beliefs and perspectives of practitioners. They ask whether it is possible to move from a mechanistic view of practice to a 'weave' of contemplative practice that encourages risk-taking and a determination of what quality means.

Section 2 examines quality improvement in action and focuses upon children at the centre of practice in the contexts of children's experiences of play, children's use of technology and the importance of creativity in practice. Natalie Canning argues in Chapter 5 that the roots of quality need to be cultivated to engage in a process of emerging quality play. She proposes eight quality principles for play to support practitioners in recognising the importance of children's autonomy and empowerment in play. In Chapter 6 Linda Tyler argues that children are already empowered in the use of technology and that practitioners need to recognise children as a new generation of 'digital citizens' or 'digizens'. Not only does she illustrate how children seamlessly use technology in their play and learning, she also warns that practitioners and settings cannot afford to be left behind. In the last chapter of this section Rosie Walker asks us to consider ways to change, how we perceive learning environments and consider opportunities for creativity. Quality in this section is in part determined by localised needs and perspectives and a focus on ways in which individual practitioners can influence quality.

In Section 3 we consider quality improvement in relation to professional practice. Developing an individual perspective on quality improvement and change does not mean negating national aspirations for quality, as arguably they complement each other. This is especially valid in considering ways to safeguard the welfare of children. Here we must learn from reviews of practice and mistakes made, and consider new ways of working, something that Claire Majella Richards explores in Chapter 8. She makes a strong case for developing 'supervision' as part of quality improvement to protect children and this is something that is now becoming embedded into practice as a consequence of serious case reviews. Positive professional change is also endorsed in Chapter 9 by Rory McDowall Clark and Sue Baylis, who consider ways to improve quality through practice-based training that extends and develops practitioner thinking in terms of leading and developing practice. In Chapter 10 Michael Reed and Alison Murphy make the case for parental partnerships in professional practice and make direct reference to the career histories of two practitioners who are at the forefront of promoting quality in practice. They consider the changing nature of family life and the impact this has on children's experiences. They suggest that reflection on practice is necessary when responding to change and ways of working with parents. This also means changing the way we approach training and qualifications, and in Chapter 11 Carla Solvason argues the need to model the quality we expect to see in practice in courses and training. She describes building 'a team around the student' and considers ways to forge communities of supportive practice that are not just for the duration of a course of study.

In each of the sections the chapters argue that quality improvement and change is an ongoing process and the book should be seen as supporting an understanding of quality that reflects positive professional change that extends and develops practitioner thinking, rather than acting as the basis for measuring quality. We suggest that quality improvement is a question of accountability, as opposed to regulation, where quality is maintained and reviewed as part of continuing professional development. We recognise that quality will mean different things in different settings and to different practitioners, and consequently advocate that what works for one might not be the best approach for another. Finally, we need a well-trained workforce, who are encouraged to develop their own reflection on practice and who have the ability to challenge and change what goes on. We contend that we now have a workforce that is able to do this through leading practice, having the confidence to voice opinions and being proactive in identifying areas of change. This supports the notion that quality improvement is about considering what practitioners do well and continuing to improve it.

Our position as editors is, of course, influenced by our own background, culture, values and beliefs and these are reflected in the content of the book. We see quality being developed as part of a professional responsibility to children and families; this may seem to be stating the obvious, but it is an important view that resonates in all the chapters. This builds upon what can be termed 'professional dispositions', where professional qualities are valued over professional competencies. We see practitioners engaged in quality improvement as being able to do what they have always done, but perhaps now more than ever understand the need for quality and recognise and celebrate the qualities they have. Quality practice is evident in everyday routines, but as such it is important to recognise these aspects and identify where they can be developed to further support children's experiences. For example, practitioners need to recognise how they:

- reflect on practice and consider different professional groups, parents and children's views;

- effectively communicate with others;

- act ethically and professionally in any form of quality improvement review that takes place;

- view child development, the way children are taught, and how they learn as well as what they learn;

- safeguard children's welfare;

- lead practice, share expertise and act as a critical friend to others;

- understand and apply aspects of diversity and inclusion to promote the welfare of children;

- use enquiry and investigation to improve quality and provide access to that quality for disadvantaged groups;

- understand the importance of developing a positive learning environment and are careful and sensitive in the way they explore the environment;

- view continuing professional development as an important aspect of professional practice for themselves and others;

- engage in work-based investigation to improve quality, reflect on practice and challenge practice.

All these statements represent much more than 'things' that are done or 'competencies' that are demonstrated. They indicate the way practitioners are continuously and actively involved in improving quality. Of course, we acknowledge some of these are driven by adhering to procedures and regulations, but it is practitioners who are making such policies work, and as they do they are forming an identity around practice. Chapter 1 suggests that such dispositions should not be seen as yet another set of requirements. They may be refined and developed by values, beliefs, personal heritage and professional skills, but inevitably this means a degree of reflection from practitioners; consequently we argue that this should be an essential part of practice-based quality improvement. Therefore, in this book we attempt to add to the debate about quality and offer views on what constitutes effective learning and teaching as well as professional roles and responsibilities. When we do this we are not constructing truths, but applying interpretations that can be probed and reconstructed. Our position is that practitioners are the key; the more they reflect on practice, the more their collective voice will be heard to influence change and improve quality.

Section 1

Quality Improvement: Process or Product?

1

What do we mean by quality and quality improvement?

Michael Reed

Chapter overview

This chapter offers a broad introduction to the concept of quality in early childhood education and what is meant by quality improvement. It sets the scene for what follows in the remainder of the book where illustrations of quality and debates about what constitutes quality are provided about aspects of early years education. It is unable to offer a single definition of what is meant by 'quality' as this is open to interpretation and is often mitigated by variables that influence how we define and refine quality. It attempts to examine the large volume of literature surrounding quality, and the professional dispositions that also impact upon quality. It argues that these need to be understood and closely examined, which will in turn help to establish what we mean when we consider 'quality in practice'.

From professional competency to quality improvement – a journey of reflection

Quality improvement is a continuous process rather than a single event. It is a process of evaluating aspects of practice to enhance and support the well-being of children and families. It involves the whole of an early years setting and is a complement and extension to the inspection process. Importantly, it is a way of self-evaluating what goes on in order to make things better. It requires listening to the views of those most closely involved, including children, and identifying key aspects for improvement. This also involves listening to external advice, recognising internal strengths and realising that any action as a result of this process may well change what people in an organisation say and do. It is often formalised into a pattern illustrated as a cycle of questions (see Figure 1.1).

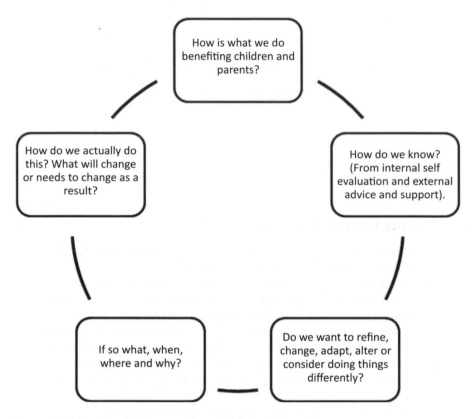

Figure 1.1 Evaluating practice to identify quality

However, this representation can be challenged as being too simplistic. In an early years setting, things are rarely so logical and focused. What happens in reality is that ideas, views, responses and challenges are a constant part of everyday life. As a consequence there is a danger that we can easily become reactive and not find the time to sit back and carefully consider what we do well and what we need to improve. There is also a danger that quality improvement is resisted. This is because in part it can be seen as being asked to refine or enact another form of 'guidance' or 'directive' from government or government agency. On the other hand, it seems that practitioners can and do welcome the responsibility of wanting to do their best for families and communities and they are willing to learn from the numerous information sources they are expected to look at. Perhaps we should see evaluating practice more like the cogs of a wheel, where answering one question leads to another and another so that a cascade of evaluation is triggered to support reflection on quality improvement (see Figure 1.2).

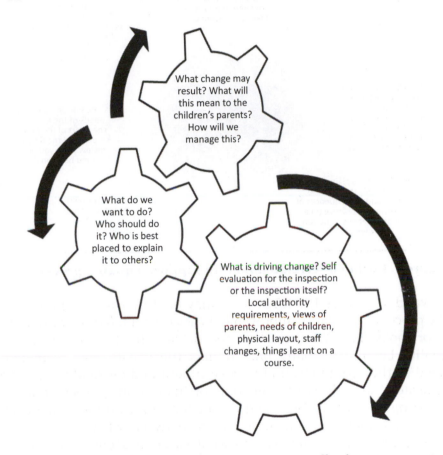

Figure 1.2 The 'cogs' of reflection to support quality improvement

Ideas for change and improvement are seldom seen on their own; they are interrelated and influence each other. We also have to prioritise and consider why doing one thing for the right reasons may well influence or have a marked impact on another part of an organisation, which can sometimes be positive but might equally be problematic. Therefore quality improvement requires less reaction, more reflection and much more evaluation and planning. It is often linked to change and the ability of practitioners to lead and manage change. It requires the skills of investigation and an understanding of 'research' processes in the workplace (Costley et al., 2010; Callan and Reed, 2011). This is because improving quality is indeed a process and not an activity that can be 'done' or 'ordered'; it requires practitioners to use all of their inherent and interrelated skills, such as those outlined in Figure 1.3.

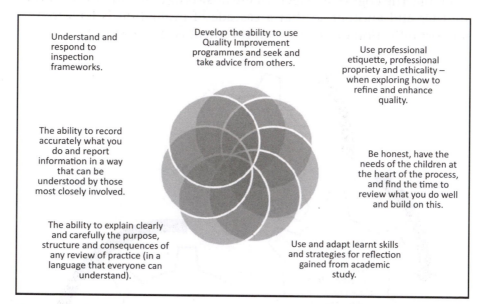

Figure 1.3 Using interrelated skills to support a quality process

As valid as Figures 1.1, 1.2 and 1.3 may be, in terms of representing the processes of quality improvement they do not tell us what 'quality' is or looks like. It is here that the debate about what constitutes quality begins. To many practitioners the debate may seem one-sided as they try to respond to government and curriculum 'quality indicators' as well as the demands of inspections, which result in a setting seen as having 'good or outstanding features'. The debate asks practitioners to somehow choose between what they in their local context see as quality and what external agencies, regulatory bodies and researchers see as quality. The debate also encompasses how children learn, and how best they can be encouraged to learn, and has yet to reach a conclusion. It has always fascinated writers, researchers, psychologists, teachers, parents and policy-makers. It has also captivated philosophers, spiritual leaders and those who study the social world of the child and family. The result has been an intense study of child development over many decades, which we would suggest is well explained by a detailed review of the research literature (Evangelou et al., 2009). We recommend reading the whole review but have selected some examples that start to tell us what quality experiences aid children's development:

- Children's development is dependent upon a wide range of interrelated factors.

- Developmental theories have been linear, with children said to follow similar pathways to adulthood, but new theories assume that development proceeds in a web of multiple strands, with different children following different pathways.

- Children are born without a sense of self; they establish this through interactions with others (adults, siblings and peers) and with their culture.

- Children thrive in warm, positive relationships.

- Play is a prime context for development.

- Conversation is a prime context for development of children's language, and also their emotions.

- Narrative enables children to create a meaningful personal and social world, but it also is a 'tool for thinking'.

- The early years curriculum needs to provide opportunities for problem-solving to develop logical mathematical thinking.

- Children's self-regulation requires the development of opportunities, which facilitates the internalisation of social rules.

- Cultural niches and repertoires are important considerations in shaping the context of children's learning.

- The concept of children's 'voice' is not new but has become an increasing focus of research.

- Enhancing children's development is skilful work, and practitioners need training and professional support.

- The quality of both the home learning environment and the setting have measurable effects on children's development.

- Quality includes relationships and interactions, but also pedagogical structures and routines for learning.

- Formative assessment is at the heart of providing a supporting and stimulating environment.

- Professional development is important for practitioners, as is liaison with agencies outside the setting.

- New research has focused on the benefits of using technology and their use in communicating between the setting and home.

This gives us our first glance at what is meant by quality. Nevertheless, it only represents the findings from a review, however sophisticated. As it suggests, there are many interrelated and complex factors that come into play when considering the way children grow and develop, and as for defining the 'best way' that might lead to 'best quality' there are certainly no easy answers.

Defining quality, explaining quality, demonstrating quality: no easy answers

Quality is influenced by our own perspectives on learning as well as by what we have read, observed and practised. We are also influenced by our position in a particular early years context or landscape. Sometimes we may be insiders operating and reflecting in an early years setting. At other times we are outsiders looking at what goes on through the eyes of what is expected by regulation or any other determinant of what is thought to be good practice. This is what Katz (1994) describes as seeing things from different perspectives, be this a parent, practitioner or visitor. This view is refined by Armistead (2008) who uses the terms 'insider' and 'outsider' in developing an argument about using children's voices as determinants of quality. To this we can add differing interpretations or theories proposed by early education pioneers such as Rousseau through to Montessori and Piaget through to Vygotsky (Mooney, 2000; Robinson, 2008). They all observed children and reached quite varied conclusions about how children learn and how adults promote learning. Their views are influential and have contributed to the design of early years curriculum frameworks in all nations of the United Kingdom.

Views about quality also come from researchers such as Taguchi (2010), who provides ideas that prompt us to consider and reconsider the way children learn and the interactivity between the world around us. Such views open up further debate by encouraging us to reflect, learn and challenge what we know and think. For example,

Dahlberg et al. (2007) and Dahlberg and Moss (2008) offer a view of quality that challenges assumptions about the term, what it means and how it can be seen. Dahlberg et al. (2007: 106) see the present and dominant 'discourse of quality' with the 'discourse of meaning making' requiring dialogue and critical reflection grounded in concrete human experiences and recognising that we all see the world from differing positions and contexts. They put forward a thought-provoking series of arguments that underline a view that people have different views of what educational outcomes should be considered as quality, and how they are reached. This differs from the body of knowledge about quality that predominates, much of it emanating from the USA. It suggests that quality practice and provision can be examined in terms of its longer-term effects on children's learning and development and that it revolves around those aspects that can be monitored, changed and imposed by regulators and government.

Myers (2005) provides a summary of these positions from the perspective of emergent and emerging economies and argues that quality early learning is based upon evidence from scientific positions that see quality as inherent in practice, identifiable and universal. He suggests that quality experiences have a pronounced effect on children's language and cognitive development but also involve effects on social development and behaviour. Although children may benefit, there is evidence that disadvantaged children may profit the most and the quality of the structure of organisations has an effect on outcomes. He recognises that although high quality is important it is also possible to find significant and even dramatic effects of programmes that are of minimal quality, judged by standards of the minority world. We should therefore see quality as being debated on a much wider front than northern Europe and the USA. For example, the work of Tikly and Barrett (2007: 15) considers quality measures related to sub-Saharan Africa and they assert that any 'understanding of education quality must consider local realities and be related to analysis of how the broader historical, socio-economic, political and cultural context interacts with educational processes'. We need to remember that contextual factors are important locally, nationally and internationally and the quality of the relationship between settings and families needs to be consciously developed as part of quality improvement. Quality should also be seen in relation to promoting access to early childhood support and therefore having quality in place without access for disadvantaged groups is not productive.

Sylva and Roberts (2010) provide a view of the methods of observing and measuring quality and its longer-term effects. The research considers health and growth, social and emotional development, and cognitive and educational development in a range of settings including care by grandparents, other relations or friends, and care by nannies or childminders. The research looks at the more subtle aspects of quality, for example gender, as well as such aspects as the relationship between a mother or caregiver and the child. It is based in the UK and therefore offers an alternative perspective to research from the USA where standards and types of provision are different. It also considers outcomes for children and probes deeply into the complexities of how those come about and what they mean. This takes us to a consideration of quality in terms of regulation and inspection. One view would be that regulation and inspection are in place solely to monitor policies and directives, but another is that regulation and inspection act in the interests of children and offer a clear basis for improvement. This perspective exposes even more debate about the way in which quality is seen and regulated (Jones, 2010). It is unlikely that many would reject the importance of employment law, anti-discriminatory legislation, health and safety, data collection regulations, legislation regarding special educational needs, safeguarding, child protection, or a duty of care. As to whether these directly act upon quality or are an ingredient of promoting quality is again part of an ongoing debate.

It is impossible to ignore the value placed upon implementing regulations and therefore we have to take into account practitioner training and professional development based upon the premise that this leads to increased expertise. Consequently, the whole notion of professional quality encompasses the very nature of professionalism and new professional roles. Engaging in reflective practice and professional development, as well as being proactive to changes in management and leadership approaches, is an essential part of early years practice. In striving to represent quality in practice the following questions acknowledge the need for personal reflection in ongoing professional practice:

• Which learning and teaching approaches are most beneficial to children?

• How do we recognise the important role of the adult in children's lives?

• Is one view of quality better than another?

There are no easy answers, only varied and different perspectives, but what we can say is there are some common features that represent the foundations of quality provision. They should not be seen as criteria that have to be met or judged in order to be given an award of 'quality'; rather they should stimulate debate and ask practitioners to think about their relevance in a world that is constantly changing. These common features require practitioners to engage in the debate about quality, to agree or disagree, change and modify, but importantly to reflect on the very idea of what is meant by quality. They can be listed as follows:

- Being a child is a very important part of life and something to cherish. It should not be seen solely as a preparation for the future.

- The environment interacts with the child so is itself something that promotes learning.

- Each child is unique, with individual ways of learning.

- Seeing the child as a 'whole child', where learning is holistic and interrelated.

- The young child does not separate experiences into different compartments.

- How a child learns is as important as what they are learning.

- Curriculum frameworks are just that – frameworks.

- Learning how to learn encourages children's self-direction, where all learning contexts, both formal and informal, are important.

- The environment should contain 'favourable conditions' for growing, learning, experimenting, listening and speaking.

- Providing opportunities for learning is as important as providing activities.

- Listening to parents and their needs.

- Young children learn through exploration, play, taking risks and accepting that there are challenges and problems to solve.

- A starting point for supporting learning is what children can do, what they can nearly do and how they learn.

- Children are now part of a digital nation, if not a digital world.

- Equality means having an equal chance to succeed.

- Listening to the voice of the child.

- Practitioners need to develop a professional voice and act ethically.

- Reflecting on practice is an essential part of professional development and consequently the development of children.

- Promoting access to early childhood support.

We are sure you will be able to challenge, add to, or delete some of these statements. Quality is an interrelated complex web that has strands that touch leadership, pedagogical understanding, personality, relationships, warmth, kindness, love, fear, concern for others, fairness and an adherence to values, that tell us that children and what we provide for them is important. Quality is not a separate entity with a starting point and an end point. It includes the way children's services are integrated and the culture that surrounds the community, as well as the experience of practitioners. There are also government reports, curriculum frameworks and analysis from the inspection process and research evidence such as the EPPE project (Sylva et al., 2004). None of these elements should be discounted or left unshared, as quality improvement is about reflecting on the whole of practice, accepting some, challenging others and making changes for the better.

Quality and professional change

Change in regulation and professional roles have undoubtedly taken place since 2000. These developments have been driven by changes in social and economic policies to meet the needs of a changing society (Maplethorpe et al., 2010). There are ongoing debates about the merits of implementing particular curriculum frameworks, let alone their content, and there have also been debates about the value of engaging in reflective practice and the importance of professional development as well as changes in and leadership and professionalisation of the workforce (Aubrey, 2007; Murray, 2009; Moss, 2008, 2010; Nurse,

2007; Pound, 2008; Miller and Cable, 2011). We have certainly seen a significant movement towards 'professionalising' the workforce and a range of qualifications and directives detailing the practice-based expectations placed upon practitioners. While these may be well intended, there is a danger that this can result in a mechanistic view of early years practice. We prefer to think more in terms of the qualities and 'professional dispositions' that can be seen in practice, such as having a caring attitude, valuing early education, reflecting carefully on the way children learn, gaining relevant qualifications and showing a desire to change practice (Rike and Sharp, 2008). They are laudable aspects of early years professionalism; however, just listing descriptors can be seen as yet another functional set of competencies and professional objectives or a set of 'requirements' that can somehow be taught. Instead, we suggest that they should be seen as dispositions that may be refined and developed by a considered exploration of values, beliefs, attributes, professional and personal heritage and professional competencies. This moves away from the notion of practitioners being seen as 'implementers' of policies, competencies and technical skills (Moss, 2010).

Moss suggests that we need to redefine practitioners' roles and sees this as a political and ethical choice that needs to start with critical questions about how the work of an early years practitioner is understood and what values are considered important. Osgood (2009) considers the opportunities available for alternative constructions of professionalism to take shape from within communities of early years practice. Others discuss the whole notion of what we mean by professionalism and identify that although we may well see change as improving quality, constant change can leave practitioners thinking that however much they strive to improve, they are not somehow meeting quality standards (Lloyd and Hallet, 2010; Osgood, 2010). Added to this is the elephant in the setting, which is the wider issue of pay, service conditions and status of the workforce (Cooke and Lawton, 2008). Similarly, there is continued tension in professional hierarchies such as in the ambiguity of early years qualifications in relation to Qualified Teacher Status. This does little to enhance quality because it is clear that practitioners need to gain qualifications that cross professional boundaries and think outside their own 'defined role' (Wenger, 2010). Thinking critically and taking a reflective stance that incorporates a holistic overview of children's services requires personal confidence and motivation to construct an interpretation of what it means for individuals to work in a particular context (Appleby, 2010). We see this as important in enabling practitioners to determine where they 'fit' in terms of contributing to early years change and development. Claxton (2003) views this as a never-ending 'learning journey' involving personal and professional qualities that merge as we develop a personal sense of responsibility and share our knowledge to forge a community or 'landscape of practice' (Wenger, 1998; Wenger et al., 2002). In this way quality can represent a balance between using indicators, targets and competencies and adding locally derived responses that encourage self-evaluation and reflection on quality.

There are established organisations that promote quality improvement. The Labour government and National Children's Bureau (NCB) established a national peer support network in 2007 called the National Quality Improvement Network (NQIN), made up of representatives drawn from local authorities and national organisations. The NCB also published a set of 'good practice principles' and guidance that links to other quality improvement initiatives. In addition, individual quality assurance schemes operate to maintain quality across the early years sector. As to the effectiveness of such programmes, Mooney (2007) provides a detailed review of diversity of provision and the impact of quality improvement programmes. She suggests that there is evidence that quality provision can have an impact on children's development and can lead to improvements in the overall quality of provision, through her evaluation of longitudinal studies from the UK and USA. However, wider indicators than direct research evidence need to be used to consider the impact of quality improvement programmes: for example, economic factors and the value of training. Interestingly, Mooney's study reveals that self-evaluation is a critical element of a quality improvement programme because it encourages reflective practice, provoking discussion and raising awareness. Importantly, it was found that quality improvement programmes did motivate practitioners and helped them to perceive the whole process of improvement and change as important.

In practice, many of these attributes can be seen in Quality Together, a quality improvement programme from Birmingham City Council (2009). The programme itself was developed using expertise from practitioners and from those representing different agencies. It underpins values and beliefs about children's play, diversity, inclusion and children's rights and is intended to assist settings in raising the quality of the service they provide. It incorporates the Early Years Quality Improvement and Support Programme (EYQISP) and is directly related to the four principles of the Early Years Foundation Stage (EYFS) in England. It is currently developing a process for settings to compose 'online' summaries of their ongoing quality improvement. Settings are asked, as they engage in developing quality, to reflect on practice and to document their own reflective journeys using evidence from their own practice. In particular, practitioners are asked to provide evidence that represents how the setting perceives quality experiences for children and families. The programme promotes self-evaluation and asks settings to consider responses to questions rather than meet a series of competencies. It also embeds training and professional development into the programme via a process of support and higher education accreditation. It therefore contains many of the determinants of quality improvement that have been exposed in this chapter.

Summary

Quality is in the first instance difficult to define. There are indeed many views on the subject, which makes it quite difficult to unpack and understand. This is because of the many variables that come into play, which range from questions about what children need to grow and develop, to evaluating the impact of the curriculum, leadership and professional roles. There are those who see practitioners at the heart of quality improvement and consider their ability to reflect on their own and their setting's practice as being important. Others argue that regulation does not produce quality and that the values and beliefs of practitioners are more important. However, it is also true that guidance, direction and support matter. Therefore, there is some common agreement starting to emerge in a recognition that quality improvement is important, but equally how we *define* quality, and how we *promote* quality is central to practice.

References

Appleby, K. (2010) 'Reflective thinking, reflective practice', in M. Reed and N. Canning (eds), *Reflective Practice in the Early Years*. London: Sage.

Armistead, J. (2008) *A Study of Children's Perspectives on the Quality of their Experiences in Early Years Provision*, PhD thesis. University of Northumbria at Newcastle: School of Health Community and Education Studies.

Aubrey, C. (2007) *Leading and Managing in the Early Years*. London: Sage.

Birmingham City Council (2009) *Quality Together: Quality Improvement Programme*. Birmingham: Birmingham City Council.

Callan, S. and Reed, M. (2011) 'Introduction', in S. Callan and M. Reed (eds), *Work-Based Research in the Early Years*. London: Sage.

Claxton, G. (2003) *The Intuitive Practitioner: On the Value of Not Always Knowing What One is Doing*. Maidenhead: Open University Press.

Cooke, G. and Lawton, K. (2008) *For Love or Money: Pay, Progression and*

Professionalization in the Early Years Workforce. London: Institute for Public Policy Research.

Costley, C., Elliott, G. and Gibbs, P. (2010) *Doing Work Based Research: Approaches to Enquiry for Insider-Researchers*. London: Sage.

Dahlberg, G. and Moss, P. (2008) 'Beyond quality in early childhood education and care', *CESifo DICE Report*, (6) 2: 21– 26, Institute for Economic Research at the University of Munich.

Dahlberg, G., Moss, P. and Pence, A. (2007) *Beyond Quality in Early Childhood Education and Care: Postmodern Perspectives* (2nd edition). London: Falmer Press.

Evangelou, M., Sylva, K., Kyriacou, M., Wild, M. and Glenny, G. (2009) *Early Years Learning and Development Literature Review*. Nottingham: DCSF.

Jones, C. (2010) 'Inspecting and evaluating the quality and standards of early years and childcare provision', in G. Pugh and B. Duffy (eds) *Contemporary Issues in the Early Years* (5th edition). London: Sage.

Katz, L. (1994) 'Perspectives on the quality of early childhood programs', *Phi Delta Kappan*, 76 (3): 200–5.

Lloyd, E. and Hallet, E. (2010) 'Professionalising the early childhood workforce in England: work in progress or missed opportunity?', *Contemporary Issues in Early Childhood*, 11 (1): 75–88.

Maplethorpe, N., Chanfreau, J., Philo, D. and Tait, C. (2010) *Families with Children in Britain: Findings from the 2008 Families and Children Study (FACS)*. London: DWP and National Centre for Social Research.

Miller, L. and Cable, C. (eds) (2011) *Professionalization, Leadership and Management in the Early Years*. London: Sage.

Mooney, A. (2007) *Effectiveness of Quality Improvement Programmes*. London: Thomas Coram Research Unit and Institute of Education, University of London.

Mooney, C.G. (2000) *Theories of Childhood: An Introduction to Dewey, Montessori, Erikson, Piaget and Vygotsky*. St Paul, MN: Redleave Press.

Moss, P. (2008) 'Foreword', in A. Paige-Smith and A. Craft (eds), *Developing Reflective Practice in the Early Years*. Maidenhead: Open University Press.

Moss, P. (2010) 'We cannot continue as we are: the educator in an education for survival', *Contemporary Issues in Early Childhood*, 11 (1): 8–19.

Murray, J. (2009) 'Value based leadership and management', in A. Robins and S. Callan (eds), *Managing Early Years Settings*. London: Sage.

Myers, R.G. (2005) 'In Search of Quality in Programmes of Early Childhood Care and Education', A paper prepared for the 2005 EFA Global Monitoring Report: Early Childhood Care and Education (ECCE).

National Quality Improvement Network (NQIN) (2007) *Quality Improvement Principles: A Framework for Local Authorities and National Organisations to Improve Quality Outcomes for Children and Young People*. London: National Children's Bureau.

Nurse, A. (2007) *The New Early Years Professional: Dilemmas and Debates*. London: David Fulton.

Osgood, J. (2009) 'Childcare workforce reform in England and "the early years professional": a critical discourse analysis', *Journal of Education Policy*, 24 (6): 733–51.

Osgood, J. (2010) 'Deconstructing "professionalism" in the nursery', in L. Miller and C. Cable (eds), *Professional Issues, Leadership and Management in the Early Years*. London: Sage.

Pound, L. (2008) 'Exploring leadership: roles and responsibilities of the early years professional', in A. Paige-Smith and A. Craft (eds), *Developing Reflective Practice in the Early Years*. Maidenhead: Open University Press.

Rike, C. and Sharp, L.K. (2008) 'Assessing pre-service teachers' dispositions: a critical dimension of professional preparation', *Childhood Education*, 84 (3): 150–3.

Robinson, M. (2008) *Child Development from Birth to Eight: A Journey through the Early Years*. Maidenhead: Open University Press.

Sylva, K. and Roberts, F. (2010) 'Quality in early childhood education: evidence for long-term effects', in G. Pugh and B. Duffy (eds), *Contemporary Issues in the Early Years* (5th edition). London: Sage.

Sylva, K., Mehuish, E., Sammons, P., Siraj-Blatchford, I. and Taggart, B. (2004) *The Effective Provision of Pre-school Education (EPPE) Project: Findings from Pre-school to End of Key Stage 1*. London: DfES.

Taguchi, H.L. (2010) *Going Beyond the Theory/Practice Divide in Early Childhood Education: Introducing an Intra-active Pedagogy*. London: Routledge.

Tikly, L. and Barrett, A. (2007) *Education Quality: Research Priorities and Approaches in the Global Era*, EdQual working paper 10. Bristol: University of Bristol. Available at: http://www.edqual.org/publications/workingpaper/edqualwp10.pdf (last accessed 12 January 2011).

Wenger, E. (1998) *Communities of Practice: Learning, Meaning and Identity*. Cambridge: Cambridge University Press.

Wenger, E. (2010) 'Landscapes of Practice', a series of workshops held at the Practice-based Professional Learning Centre for Excellence in Teaching and Learning. Milton Keynes: Open University.

Wenger, E., McDermott, R. and Snyder, W. (2002) *Cultivating Communities of Practice*. Cambridge, MA: Harvard Business School Press.

2

Childminding: an essential part of quality childcare in the community

Michael Reed with Sue Owen

Chapter overview

This chapter explores childminding provision, which forms a significant part of early years practice in the UK. It argues that there is no simple illustration of what quality childminding looks like; however, we can learn from research evidence surrounding childminding and start to understand how quality is perceived by childminders themselves and the families who use their services. It highlights the importance of childminding networks in the development of quality provision and explores the unique qualities of childminding. It also reveals tensions about childminders having to meet 'outside' requirements exemplified by regulation and curriculum design while responding to the needs of parents in the community using their own 'insider' knowledge. We suggest that 'quality childminding' is more than demonstrating a professional adherence to the curriculum or regulations, and recognise that quality improves with engagement in training, collaboration with others and reflection on how to improve practice. Childminding, then, provides a professional home-based learning environment, which is understood and accessible to parents, gives personal attention to children, while providing warmth, security and continuity of care. This gives childminding its unique place in the sector.

What do we mean by childminding: home care or something more?

In England in 2009 there were 51,000 active childminders, compared with 103,000 childcare and early years providers (Phillips et al., 2010). This tells us that childminding is a significant part of early years provision and has an important place in the early years sector. The Office for Standards in Education (Ofsted) in England defines a childminder as 'someone who provides care for children to whom they are not related and of any age up to their 18th birthday on domestic premises for reward' (Ofsted, 2010a). They go on to provide detailed advice about the requirements that need to be in place in order to become a childminder and the way in which childminders are inspected. This usually takes place within seven months of starting to care for children and then at least once every three or four years. Inspectors consider how childminders organise their service and how they promote continuous improvement to enhance quality. Childminders are expected to follow a specified curriculum framework to promote learning; as part of the inspection process they are rated as unsatisfactory, satisfactory, good, or outstanding. The National Childminding Association (NCMA) is the leading body representing and supporting childminders and suggests that childminding is the preferred form of childcare in England and rated highly by parents. They argue that childminding is much more than providing learning opportunities, because childminders give focused support, valuing children and their unique qualities (NCMA, 2010).

In Wales, a childminder must register with the Care and Social Services Inspectorate Wales (CSSIW) before they can start childminding, and attend a pre-registration (briefing) session. They must also meet minimum standards for childminding and the childminding and day care regulations (WAG, 2002) and formal checks on their suitability to work with children are carried out. Most recently, there has been some debate over new requirements which mean that care for children aged eight and over taking place for less than two hours or between 6 p.m. and 2 a.m. is not covered by regulation. However, the intention is to promote flexibility and choice rather than restrict such things as babysitting (Lepper, 2010). Unlike England, there is no grading system in Wales for childminder inspections. But in Scotland there are similar checks, which include references, a health assessment, and a police check on the potential childminder and every other adult over 16 in their household (SCMA, 2010). The potential childminder's home is inspected to ensure that it is a safe and suitable environment for children and thereafter there is an annual inspection. It is useful to read what advice the Scottish Commission for the Regulation of Care (2010: 2) gives to childminders about an impending inspection:

> We recognise that although day care services and childminders work with children in the same age group, they provide different services, each with their own unique strengths. We don't compare the two nor expect them to be run in the same way. The most important thing is that, irrespective of the service type, the needs of children are being met and the outcomes for children are the best they can be.

This immediately tells us that childminding in Scotland is recognised as having special features and that childminders are encouraged to focus on the way children are at the heart of what they do. Further support is available from the Scottish Childminding Association (SCMA). It suggests that childminding, like any other childcare occupation, requires a clear induction to the role and responsibilities involved, and the SCMA has developed a programme to help childminders understand what is required in establishing a home-based childcare and education service. The programme is delivered in a series of interactive sessions adopting a group discussion format. Where possible, this programme runs in conjunction with Care Commission representation, which has been agreed nationally. There is also a national training framework which offers childminders the opportunity to evidence their level of occupational competency by reflecting on and evaluating current working practice in line with national care standards.

In Northern Ireland a childminder must register with the local Health and Social Services Trust and meet defined standards to do with safety, equipment, and numbers of children. Following on from registration, childminders are inspected annually by the Health and Social Services Trust (NICMA, 2008). These requirements tell us that all the nations in the UK insist upon careful scrutiny of those wishing to become childminders; they also recognise how training can influence practice and impose a rigorous inspection framework.

We can say, therefore, that in all nations of the UK childminders are at work in the community. They are all regulated, they have to adhere in some way to curriculum requirements, be checked as to their suitability, and show due regard for children's safety and welfare. In addition governments, assemblies and parliaments, when providing advice to prospective and established childminders, cite quality as an important part of provision. For example, in England Ofsted provide ten questions for childminders to consider when developing best practice. They indicate what quality features are seen as important and ask questions that require a degree of reflection on practice. The questions are as follows (Ofsted, 2009: 15):

1   When did you last update your knowledge of the Local Safeguarding Children Board guidance?
2   How well do children understand and manage risks to themselves?
3   How well does your planning take account of children's starting points and interests?
4   How effective is the balance between adult-led and child-directed learning?
5   How well can children play freely indoors and outdoors?
6   How well do you help parents and carers to support their children's learning?
7   How effectively do you work with parents and carers on a daily basis to make sure that children's needs are addressed?
8   How successfully do you include all children and families in the opportunities available?
9   How well does your self-evaluation include the views of parents, carers, children and other professionals?
10 How involved are you in regular networks, training or programmes of study to extend your knowledge about childcare and development?

These questions tell us that childminders are seen as a professional part of the early years sector, but they also assume that opportunities exist for childminders to avail themselves of training which is not always that easy to access. The questions also start to narrow the focus towards 'curriculum and quality' rather than a wider, flexible community response. They do, however, mirror some aspects of the NCMA (2006) *Charter for Quality in Childminding*, which provides a focus on practice. NCMA's Quality Standards, listed on their website, suggest that childminders should take a professional approach to:

* managing children's behaviour

* promoting equality of opportunity

* respecting confidentiality

* promoting children's learning and development

* working in partnership with parents

- keeping children safe

- knowing about nutrition

- having good business practices

- seeking support.

The charter contains essential points about what constitutes a framework for quality and encompasses what many government agencies and research evidence suggest: that there are positive correlations between quality provision, children's attainment and the level of practitioner qualifications and knowledge (Sylva et al., 2004). The NCMA website also articulates beliefs about home-based childcare (About NCMA: NCMA's Beliefs). These are interesting as they begin to tell us about the values and 'qualities' inherent in childminding, which are inevitably linked to professional competencies and quality of provision. NCMA says that children benefit because childminding is:

- Consistent – a child is cared for by the same registered childminder or nanny each day, often over a number of years.

- Flexible – a registered childminder or nanny can care for a child whose parents work atypical hours and can provide full, as well as wraparound, childcare.

- Inclusive – a registered childminder or nanny can care for children of different ages and abilities together in family groups.

- Community-focused – a registered childminder or nanny can reflect the needs of local communities and enable the children they care for to be part of their local community.

- Personalised – a registered childminder or nanny can meet the needs of individual children and families such as teen parents or disabled children.

- Supportive – babies and younger children, especially, do best in home-based childcare because they are cared for in smaller groups and by the same registered childminder or nanny each day.

All of this indicates that a potential childminder needs to have more than an abiding interest in working with children. They have to adhere to regulation, understand curriculum frameworks and be prepared to reflect on their own practice. There are a number of different and differing views on what makes a good childminder; however, there are some common features that represent quality. These include training, reflection, community response, diversity, responsiveness to parents, flexibility and the ability to think beyond the curriculum. These are, of course, broad terms and the actual specifics of childminding quality still remain to a large extent elusive. What we do know is that childminding is unique and it is not the same as other forms of provision. As to whether it is perceived as having the same status is an ongoing point of debate, but it is clear that any drive towards enhanced status brings with it the responsibility to engage in quality improvement strategies. Whether quality determinants should recognise the special features found in childminding is again a point for further reflection.

Perceptions of quality and provision

Varied viewpoints exist when it comes to considering quality in the early years. These come from governments and researchers, all of whom have attempted to define and articulate what and how young children should learn. This is happening worldwide, not just in the UK. Most recently the Australian government (2010) developed a comprehensive framework of monitoring and developing early childhood education projects in order to 'measure' quality, but it seems that few have concentrated on childminding. Siraj-Blatchford and Siraj-Blatchford (2009) suggest that research into childminding practice is lacking; however, quality may be enhanced when there is access to training aimed at helping childminders to provide secure, sensitive care and a high-quality learning environment. Owen (2000, 2005, 2006) reinforces this position using evidence from systematic studies of quality, in relation to different aspects of early years provision, and focuses upon childminding. Her 2006 research offers a wider view of quality, suggesting that many childminders believe that quality childminding is constructed differently from quality in group-based provision and that a more professional approach towards quality should not undermine the traditional flexibility, homeliness and 'loving' nature of their work. She argues for a re-evaluation of society's view of childminding and of what constitutes high-quality provision within a home-based setting, and underlines the value of childminding networks. These can be described as a coordinated group of registered childminders who join together to share ideas, views and experience. Through a network, childminders have access to training and to specialist advice. In addition, parents in England using an accredited network childminder can access financial support for childcare, which places childminders on par with other forms of provision.

International evidence about childminding predominately comes from the USA. Phillips (1987) found that the clearest links between childcare approaches and good child development outcomes were:

- smaller group sizes;

- caregiver training (especially in child care);

- higher general levels of provider education;

- a higher level of responsive, informative and accepting interaction with the child;

- an orderly physical environment more appropriate to children's activities;

- more opportunity to relate to older children;

- the chance for children to interact with a wide range of toys and activities.

This study also considered the idea of looking at ways in which different aspects of children's environments act upon each other. For instance, they developed a measure that combined the degree to which toys were present in the home and in the day care setting. They found that this was influential in predicting good child development outcomes. Childcare is seen as part of the child's life; as Phillips (1987: 40) suggests, 'Children do not live by child care alone – no matter how fitting its form or how fine its features.' Clarke-Stewart et al. (2002) also studied childminders' homes using data from research in a number of states in the USA. The selected childminders cared for at least two children and received payment for childcare supporting children aged between 15 and 36 months. It was found that childminders who had received higher levels of education provided interactive learning environments, sensitive care and stimulating activities that had a child-centred approach. Quality was not seen as solely related to a childminder's age, experience, professionalism, or the ratio of children to childminder. It related more to a child-centred approach and the provision of a stimulating home environment.

More recently, Vandell et al. (2010) conducted research for the National Institute of Child Health and Human Development (NICHD) that sought to determine whether early childcare quality, quantity and type could be a predictor of children's achievement and behaviour problems at age 15. They measured quality, hours and type of care during the early years, collected results of standardised tests of achievement, and obtained reports from families and schools. The children were from diverse backgrounds, and the study found that those attending high-quality care during early childhood scored higher on tests of cognitive and academic achievement than teenagers at 15 who had attended programmes with low-quality care. There are many other studies, but all appear to reinforce the point that intensive, good-quality early years environments, with well-educated practitioners, are required if all forms of early intervention (as well as childminding) are to make a substantive difference in the achievement of especially disadvantaged children.

There have also been attempts to consider quality through the use of scales assisting in evaluating family childcare environments. For example, the Family Day Care Rating Scale (FDCRS) (Harms and Clifford, 1989) was used in the United States to link aspects of family childcare practice with outcomes in terms of child development. It was followed by the Family Child Care Environment Scale (Harms et al., 2007). These scales were found to be reliable indicators of provision, although they tended to present aspects of education, development and resources separately. It is important to recognise that scales inevitably act and react on each other and on specific situations of individual practitioners and families to produce what is then experienced by children. However useful these may be, at least as an indicator on quality, they do not necessarily reflect differences in quality and may be difficult to interpret in terms of defining quality; for example, they do not consider the challenges of meeting the needs of disadvantaged communities. It is therefore important to be cautious when considering provision that is not easily measured or defined, because it can so easily be seen in a number of ways. For example, Coghlan et al. (2009) see provision as 'narrowing the gap' and viewing quality as providing access to disadvantaged groups. There are also other interpretations of quality, such as those from the *Families Childcare and Children Study* (Sylva et al., Online). The purpose of this research was to examine the short and longer term effects of childcare on children's development between birth and school entry. The research considered a number of aspects including children's health and growth, social and emotional development, and cognitive and educational development. The following types of care were studied:

- care at home by mother and/or father;

- care by grandparents, other relations, or friends;

- care by nannies in the child's own home;

- care by childminders in the childminder's home;

- group care in day nurseries or childcare centres, both public and private;

- combinations of the above.

This is a significant project and as yet there are limited conclusions to make from its findings. There are, however, some interesting views from Sylva et al., (in press) which indicate that the quantity and stability of care was found to be predictive of higher cognitive ability, and although the effect sizes were small, such modest effects are important when viewed in light of the widespread use of care during infancy and early childhood. The premise of the research itself is also important, as it allows an exploration of children's experiences and how children are cared for by others. It underlines the importance of exploring aspects of childcare and education that can be influenced and regulated by government, namely group size, staff to child ratios, training and qualifications. Hansen and Hawkes (2009) have provided evidence taken from a large sample of respondents. They used data from the UK for a sample of children in the Millennium Cohort Study, whose mothers were working when they were nine months old, to test how different forms of childcare at an early age play a role in the production of cognitive skills and the behavioural development of young children. They found that grandparent care, which has received negative attention in the past, is shown to be positively associated with some test scores and the ability to problem-solve. Whether these studies clarify the issue of what type of provision is a prerequisite of quality is still debatable, as is whether childminding can be easily 'measured' or 'compared' with other forms of provision. We are therefore starting to view quality as wider than the here and now, and seeing continuity of care as being another important variable. This suggests that quality should also be considered in the way it supports the needs of the local community and the real lives of children and families and the wider social aspects that impact on their lives.

This view of quality sits within an 'ecological' approach, developed by Bronfenbrenner (1979), which has been highly influential in offering a perspective that takes into account the social 'systems' within which children are cared for. This has encouraged researchers to look at children's lives in a holistic way, considering all the complex elements that influence children's development and life experiences. It is a view supported by Siraj-Blatchford and Siraj-Blatchford (2009: 2), who ask that we focus 'attention directly on the progress being made by individual children and to respond with whatever tools and strategies that we find to be effective to secure their future success and wellbeing'. Other studies have attempted to identify quality in childminding by listening to the voices of parents who use the service. Ferri (1992: 151) consulted with parents and childminders to determine the most commonly mentioned features of 'quality'. These included extending children's horizons, fostering social relations among children, forming an affectionate relationship with a child, and providing a safe, secure environment. Mooney and Munton (1998: 9) conducted a project to develop materials and procedures that would both monitor quality in childminding settings and assist in quality improvement. They consulted with different groups – parents, providers, local authority officers and national organisations – in order to compare researchers' conclusions with practical knowledge and needs of the four groups. From their analysis they identified nine themes of 'quality':

- affordability and accessibility

- continuity

- adaptation/transition (settling children in)

- training and qualifications of providers

- working conditions for providers

- social status of childcare

- education and curriculum

- partnership between parents and providers

- assessing and enhancing quality.

Mooney and Munton's research produced varied results. Some aspects of quality were found to be related to structural indicators or training and qualifications; some were process indicators, for example partnership with parents and being flexible; while others related to adult needs such as affordability and working conditions. As expected, not all were given equal importance by the four groups and there were mixed opinions; for instance, training was seen as less important and more problematic by childminders and the parents who used them than by regulators and advisers. Mooney et al. (2008) revealed that the way childminders perceive their role has a bearing on quality. Some childminders felt there was a lack of recognition for their work, and they were not well remunerated for their efforts; a minority felt they were not valued by parents. Whether this view was influenced by needing to adapt to curriculum changes and the demands of regulation is speculation, but it is true that childminders work with the same expectations and policy documentation as early years settings. This means that there are sometimes discrepancies between the nature of childminding as seen by policy-makers and that seen by providers and parents.

A recent annual report prepared by Ofsted continually refers to quality in the early years sector and how there have been rises and falls in quality, including childminding practice (Ofsted, 2010b). In terms of overall quality it indicates a strong correlation between participation in quality assurance schemes for all providers, and how this tends to drive forward practice. It also suggests that differences in quality between childminding and other provision may be influenced by the opportunity of working with others and being able to identify common areas for improvement. Of course, Ofsted represents a particular view of quality, which can be challenged as to its appropriateness for childminders. However, the report does recognise the qualities of childminders beyond the parameters of the inspection framework. It suggests that childminders have a clear understanding of the needs of children in the communities they serve, engage with the curriculum and put children first. Importantly, in areas with high levels of deprivation the difference in 'quality' between childminding and other forms of provision was much less.

We suggest that childminders build close and enduring relationships with families who face challenges and these extend beyond when children are present. They are trusted by parents, develop friendships and are able to respond to family concerns in a way that does not represent someone in authority. They are positive role models and encourage children to succeed. Indeed, the appreciation levels of parents has been an abiding feature of research into childminding. For example, Speight et al. (2008, 2010) found that parents chose childminders on trust; they formed positive relationships with the childminder, which proved to be significant in relation to perceptions of quality. They suggest that some families value the importance of the familiar more than others whose awareness and income might afford them choices about childcare that could be described as more rational. The Audit Commission (2010), although not specifically addressing access to childminding, found that trust and a community response were factors in involving parents, especially those who were caring for a child on their own. Blake (2010) considered the perceptions of parents from groups in the community that were usually not heard and again suggested that parents value characteristics such as trust, familiarity, safety, nearness to home and the skills of the provider.

We have a view of childminding, that recognises its important role in the community and how parents value its convenience and, importantly, the relationships forged with childminders. Where support, training, quality improvement programmes and networking occur it appears to have a positive impact on quality. As to whether regulation and changes in curriculum requirements have enhanced childminding quality is a matter of debate. What is obvious is that there has been a reduction in the number of childminders and a widening gap between those joining this part of the sector and those leaving it; however, though there has been less of a reduction in terms of overall places available for children (Ofsted 2010c). Childminders themselves seem to recognise the positive impact of training but sometimes see compliance with regulation as superseding the needs of children.

Insider and outsider perspectives on quality

Other variables offer an additional dimension to the debate, examples of which can be seen in the work of Stephen and Brown (2004) and Armistead (2008). Armistead suggests that quality can be determined by insider and outsider perspectives. She considers 'quality' as a critical aspect of early years provision and something that has multiple meanings. It is suggested that there are two main positions: an 'outsider' perspective, characterised by structure, formal processes and outcomes; and an 'insider' perspective of those working in settings, including children, for whom the daily lived experience informs a process of relationships and events with their own consequences. The terms (although broadly similar in the sense of positioning oneself on an issue or subject) should not necessarily be confused with descriptions of work-based inquiry (Costley et al., 2010). Armistead uses the outsider term in relation to outside stakeholders such as policy-makers and funders, both local and national. Insider groups are made up of practitioners, teachers, nursery nurses and childcare professionals. Academics, early years consultants and parents occupy an area in between: sometimes outsiders, but at other times having insider perspectives.

Persistently overlooked are the children receiving early years provision. They provide the key insider perspective and a different view on what constitutes quality. This helps us to challenge the orthodoxy of seeing a local community-based service measured by outsiders because insiders see it as a process emanating from their own reflective practice. These views are important when seen in the context of childminding, which has historically seen itself as being part of and supporting access to childcare in the community and having what Katz (1998) would term as a 'bottom-up' approach to provision rather than a 'top-down' perspective. This becomes more apparent when we consider childminders extending and developing networks within the community and thus building on their inherent strengths in that community. They do this by working in tandem with other agencies and having a holistic view of serving the community – especially when linked with childminding networks and children's centres (NCMA, 2004).

There is also evidence from the initial findings of the National Childminding Survey (Fauth et al., 2010), which reported that 44 per cent of respondents said that they were part of a formal childminding network or a quality improvement network. Likewise, O'Hara (2009) reviewed daycare experiences in Ireland and reinforced the view that good-quality childcare means encompassing various services, and revealed how we should consider the community needs of parents who are finding it difficult to manage a work–life balance. This practical and important issue is exemplified by a partnership between the public and voluntary sectors in Scotland. The project successfully created new childminding opportunities in areas of high deprivation, easing the overwhelming demand for quality childcare while enabling young mothers to seek employment or further education (SCR, 2009). These examples give us an idea about the diverse nature of quality childminding and tell us to look at quality from differing perspectives. If we see childminders as people with a rather narrow insider perspective and who 'care for children' then we have done childminding a disservice. What we are saying is that we recognise the personal positive dispositions of childminders, which include listening to and articulating the voices of children. Jackson (2010) identifies dispositions such as the ability to forge positive 'relationships' with parents and be someone a parent can trust. Add to this 'community involvement' and we have an interesting and different view on quality from 'insiders' who have a personalised and less regulatory perception of what quality means.

Of course, regulatory 'outside' perceptions are also important, and we make no attempt to dismiss or minimise their impact on quality. However, they may not be accessible to or understood by parents, and it may be that childminders have another important dimension of quality: the ability to comprehend the multiple languages of different professions and interpret these views for parents. It is also important to use training and development to reflect on practice, and this is shown to have a positive influence on improving quality and outcomes for children. This means that childminders need to feel that their training is appreciated by parents and valued by other agencies. Otherwise they may be disinclined to gain further qualifications (Mooney et al., 2008). However, there is also evidence that some childminders are taking advantage of training. Working with children in one's own home can be seen as much more than caring for children or an extension of what we might call 'parenting expertise'. For example, in England a recent report from Ofsted (2010c: 4) judged 9 per cent of childminders to be offering 'outstanding' Early Years Foundation Stage provision, with a further 55 per cent seen as 'good'. The report stated that outstanding providers viewed reflective practice to be 'crucial to their success'. Childminders 'look at areas of weakness and learn from mistakes . . . they think creatively and are adventurous to find and try new ways to make a positive difference'.

Fauth et al. (2010) conducted a detailed survey of childminders as part of a study of childminding practice in the twenty-first century. The initial findings tell us what many childminders consider to be important in their work and the principles on which to base good practice. It is not a coincidence, of course, that there are similarities between the elements identified in the survey and those seen by researchers as predictors of quality. However, the report is somewhat different in that it reveals in some detail how childminders perceive themselves and their roles and responsibilities. The survey sought answers to key questions about parental choice and the requirements of the curriculum, as well as parent partnerships, the way childminders perceive children's learning and the demands of the curriculum. The findings revealed that childminders worked long hours, and took less than four weeks' annual leave per year. In terms of qualifications they were less likely to view training as an important aspect of quality, preferring to value promoting a caring approach and providing a family-friendly environment. Their day-to-day activities with children were varied and included outings and visits to local community resources. As for why they became childminders, this tended to emerge from something that was convenient in relation to caring for their own children and later because of a desire to work with children.

They were in the main satisfied with their role, but least satisfied with lack of security and monetary aspects. Parents were welcomed and involved in a variety of ways, although tensions over being 'taken for granted' and being paid were raised as concerns. Those who responded to the survey tended to participate actively in childminding networks; therefore, most were knowledgeable about curriculum frameworks and were inclined to see the paperwork involved as less challenging than might be anticipated. However, those with qualifications were more confident than others about offering care to children with additional needs. The overall picture was that childminders provide flexibility, offer out-of-hours care and have a positive and 'sharing' rapport with parents. It was the administrative and financial aspects that they found challenging. Most were satisfied with their role and capable of adjusting to curriculum requirements and the regulatory gaze from government and government agencies. Those that were unaware of or unresponsive to demands for adherence to regulation exemplified the tension between care and education.

Summary

Without doubt, childminding is an important part of early years provision. The research evidence tells us that it is effective, and produces positive outcomes, especially in disadvantaged areas and with disadvantaged groups. Childminders view themselves as supporting children and families in a warm, caring and responsive way within the local community and parents view childminders as people they form relationships with and can trust. In part this is because childminders are able to help and support families to understand professional languages and requirements. Childminders are also becoming more engaged with professional networks and accessing training, which leads to improved professional practice. This is especially true when they are supported by development workers and organisations such as the NCMA, which promotes improvement from inside 'networked communities' rather than it being imposed from outside. There are clear signs that childminding is a professional part of provision and a recognition that it does more than follow a curriculum or adhere to regulations, because it makes children and families feel secure and supports them through important transitions in their lives. When there are clearer career choices for childminders and a resolution of the regulation, childminding quality will be enhanced.

References

Armistead, J. (2008) *A Study of Children's Perspectives on the Quality of their Experiences in Early Years Provision*, PhD thesis. University of Northumbria at Newcastle: School of Health Community and Education Studies.

Audit Commission (2010) *Giving Children a Healthy Start*. London: Audit Commission.

Australian Government (2010) *National Quality Framework for Early Childhood Education and Care*. Available at: http://www.deewr.gov.au/Earlychildhood/ Policy_Agenda/Quality/Pages/home.aspx (last accessed 29 December 2010).

Blake, S. (2010) *Parental Views and Experiences of Childcare in Devon*. Exeter: Devon County Council Early Years and Childcare Service.

Bronfenbrenner, U. (1979) *The Ecology of Human Development: Experiments by Nature and Design*. Cambridge, MA: Harvard University Press.

Clarke-Stewart, A., Vandell, D., Burchinal, M., O'Brien, M. and McCartney, K. (2002) 'Do regulable features of childcare homes affect children's development?', *Early Childhood Research Quarterly*, 17 (1): 52–86.

Coghlan, M., Bergeron, C., White, K., Sharp, C., Morris, M. and Rutt, S. (2009) *Narrowing the Gap in Outcomes for Young Children Through Effective Practices in the Early Years*. London: Centre for Excellence and Outcomes in Children and Young People's Services.

Costley, C., Elliott, G. and Gibbs, P. (2010) *Doing Work Based Research*: *Approaches to Enquiry for Insider-Researchers*. London: Sage.

Fauth, R., Jelicic, H., Lea, J., Owen, S. and Willmott, N. (2010) *Childminding Practice in England: Initial Survey Findings*. London: National Children's Bureau.

Ferri, E. (1992) *What Makes Childminding Work? Study of Training for Childminders*. London: National Children's Bureau.

Hansen, K. and Hawkes, D. (2009) 'Early childcare and child development', *Journal of Social Policy*, 38 (1): 211–39.

Harms, T. and Clifford, R. (1989) *Family Day Care Rating Scale*. New York: Teachers College Press.

Harms, T., Cryer, D. and Clifford, R. (2007) *Family Child Care Environment Rating Scale – Revised Edition*. New York: Teachers College Press.

Jackson, A. (2010) 'Defining and measuring quality in early years settings', in M. Reed and N. Canning (eds), *Reflective Practice in the Early Years*. London: Sage.

Katz, L. (1998) 'What can we learn from Reggio Emilia?', in C. Edwards, L. Gandini and G. Forman (eds), *The Hundred Languages of Children: The Reggio Emilia Approach to Early Childhood Education* (2nd edition). New Jersey: Norwood.

Lepper, J. (2010) 'Safeguarding concerns raised over Welsh childcare regulations', *Children and Young People Now Magazine*, 24 November.

Mooney A. and Munton, A.G. (1998) *Research and Policy in Early Childhood Services: Time for a New Agenda*. London: Institute of Education.

Mooney, A., Boddy, J., Statham, J. and Warwick, I. (2008) 'Approaches to developing health in early years settings', *Health Education*, 108 (2): 163–77.

National Childminding Association (NCMA) (2004) *Childminders and Children's Centres: Working Together NCMA Briefing*. Kent: NCMA.

National Childminding Association (NCMA) (2006) *Charter for Quality in Childminding*. Kent: NCMA.

National Childminding Association (NCMA) (2010) *Become a Registered Childminder*. Kent: NCMA.

National Childminding Association (NCMA) (no date) *Quality Standards* Available at: http://www.ncma.org.uk/about_ncma/join_ncma/types_of_membership/quality_standards.aspx (last accessed 29 December 2010).

National Childminding Association (NCMA) (no date) *About NCMA: NCMA's Beliefs*. Available at: http://www.ncma.org.uk/about_ncma.aspx (last accessed 29 December 2010).

Northern Ireland Childminding Association (NICMA) (2008) *Childminding as a Profession: A Guide to Registration*. Newtownards: NICMA.

Office for Standards in Education (Ofsted) (2009) *Childminding: A Passion to be Outstanding*. Manchester: Crown Copyright.

Office for Standards in Education (Ofsted) (2010a) *How We Inspect: Childminders*. Available at: http://www.ofsted.gov.uk/Ofsted-home/About-us/How-we-inspect/Childminders (last accessed 29 December 2010).

Office for Standards in Education (Ofsted) (2010b) *The Annual Report of Her Majesty's Chief Inspector of Education, Children's Services and Skills 2009/10*. London: The Stationery Office.

Office for Standards in Education (Ofsted) (2010c) *Registered Childcare Providers and Places at 30 September 2010*. Manchester: Crown Copyright.

O'Hara, M. (2009) 'Exploring childcare: a north west of Ireland study', *Irish Journal of Applied Social Studies*, 9 (1): 48–64.

Owen, S. (2000) 'Assessing quality in childminding', *Children and Society*, 14 (2): 147–53.

Owen, S. (2005) *Children Come First: The Role of Approved Childminding Networks in Changing Practice*. London: National Children's Bureau and National Childminding Association.

Owen, S. (2006) *Organised Systems of Childminding in Britain: A Sociological Examination of Changing Social Policies, a Profession and the Operation of a Service*, doctoral thesis. Santa Cruz: University of California.

Phillips, D.A. (1987) *Quality in Child Care: What Does Research Tell Us?* Washington, DC: NAEYC.

Phillips, R., Norden, O., McGinigal, S., Garnett, E. and Oseman, D. (2010) *2009 Childcare and Early Years Providers Survey*, Research Brief DFE-RB012. London: Department for Education.

Scottish Commission for the Regulation of Care (2010) *Childminders: What to Expect When We Inspect*. Dundee: Care Communications.

Scottish Centre for Regeneration (SCR) (2009) *The SURF Awards for Best Practice in Community Regeneration 2009*. Edinburgh: Scottish Government and Highlands and Islands Enterprise.

Scottish Childminding Association (SCMA) (2010) *How to Become a Childminder* Available at: http://www.childminding.org/become-a-childminder/how-to-become-a-childminder (last accessed 29 December 2010).

Siraj-Blatchford, I. and Siraj-Blatchford, J. (2009) *Improving Development Outcomes for Children Through Effective Practice in Integrating Early Years Services*. London: Centre for Excellence and Outcomes in Children and Young People's Services (C4EO).

Speight, S., Smith, R., La Valle, I., Schneider, V., Perry, J., Coshall, C. and Tipping, S. (2008) *Childcare and Early Years Survey of Parents*, Ref: RR136. Nottingham: DCSF and National Centre for Social Research.

Speight, S., Smith, R., Lloyd, E. and Coshall, C. (2010) *Families Experiencing Multiple Disadvantage: Their Use of and Views on Childcare Provision*, Ref: RR191. Nottingham: DCSF and National Centre for Social Research.

Stephen, C. and Brown, S. (2004) 'The culture of practice in pre-school provision: outsider and insider perspectives', *Research Papers in Education*, 19 (3): 323–44.

Sylva, K., Mehuish, E., Sammons, P., Siraj-Blatchford, I. and Taggart, B. (2004) *The Effective Provision of Pre-school Education (EPPE) Project: Findings from Pre-school to end of Key Stage 1*. London: DfES.

Sylva, K., Stein, A., Leach, P., Barnes, J. and Erik, L. (in press) 'Effects of early childcare on cognition, language and self regulation at 18 months: an English study', *British Journal of Developmental Psychology*.

Sylva, K., Stein, A. and Leach, P. (no date) *Families Childcare and Children Study*. Available at: http://familieschildrenchildcare.org/fccc_frames_home.html (last accessed 29 December 2010).

Vandell, D., Belsky, J., Burchinal, M., Steinberg, L. and Vandergraft, N. (2010) 'Do effects of early child care extend to age 15 years? Results from the NICHD study of early child care and youth development', *Child Development*, 81 (3): 737–56.

Welsh Assembly Government (WAG) (2002) *National Minimum Standards for Childminders*. Cardiff: Welsh Assembly Government.

3

Quality improvement: integrated working

Michael Reed and Parm Sansoyer

Chapter overview

We can remember a time when there was little in the form of an early years curriculum. Practitioners were seldom required to consider children's holistic development or who else they might work with, including parents. Today integrated working is a central focus of the early years curriculum, regulation and inspection. This requires policies to be in place to ensure that practitioners protect and safeguard the welfare of children by liaising with others, and there is an expectation that professionals work together. It is therefore important that professional groups should strive to implement 'joined-up working'. This chapter examines a changing landscape of professional practice and asks whether such a drive towards working together can improve quality. We acknowledge the dilemmas and contradictions surrounding integrated working as part of quality improvement initiatives, and argue that policy and regulation have driven forward integrated working. We also suggest that however much regulation informs and develops practice, it is practitioners who make this work.

A culture of change: towards integrated working

Practitioners today are expected to consider the 'whole child' and their learning needs as part of a defined curriculum framework. They are asked to work in partnership with parents and expected to promote children's well-being. They are expected to share information with others and work with professionals from other agencies. Such expectations are found in all the nations of the UK (Reed and Canning, 2009) and they have been developed via a range of initiatives, or what we call 'contributing factors', which are playing a part in developing integrated working. These are shown as Figure 3.1.

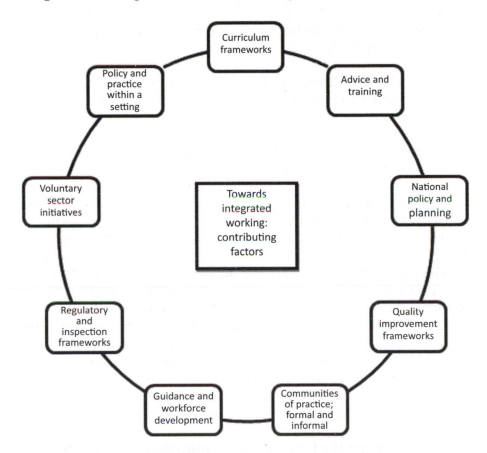

Figure 3.1 – Towards integrated working: contributing factors

Figure 3.1 illustrates the driving factors contributing to integrated working and it is essential that these are seen as interrelated, because each one overlaps and impacts upon the other. When taken together they provide a strong message about the 'forces' promoting integrated working and by implication the value placed upon integrated working. Let us look at how they operate. There are regulatory and inspection frameworks that ask inspectors to carefully consider if integrated practice is developing in settings for the benefit of children and families. They also consider the implementation of early years curriculum frameworks, which in all the nations of the UK include integrated working as an essential part of the curriculum and a means of offering continuity and progression for children's learning, as well as developing coordinated access to services. For the settings themselves there are policies and practices that are the mainstay of implementing national policies and directives. It is here that we may see local innovation as a driving force. Such innovations are usually generated *from* practice and *for* practice, which helps to forge communities of practice between practitioners and professional groups at a local level.

There are also coordinated strategies that ask practitioners to work together in order to protect vulnerable children. An example of this is the Common Assessment Framework (CAF) (CWDC, 2007). This system was developed in order to improve the effectiveness of multi-agency working by establishing common processes for assessment and information-sharing to assist the monitoring of vulnerable children. Government workforce development organisations, established to promote integrated working and influence the content of training courses are another driving force. They take a variety of forms in the UK; some directly emanate from government, some represent the voluntary sector and others are statutory agencies. For example, Children in Scotland is a national agency for voluntary, statutory and professional organisations and individuals working with children and their families. Such bodies all promote the need for integrated working. There is also the voluntary sector itself. This sector influences actions in practice, lobbies for action nationally and locally supports training; it has a direct impact on families and other professional groups. The sector is also positioned to support or challenge national policies, plans and directives that are developed to influence and support integrated working.

Also important are the training and qualification requirements that emanate from government. They ask that early childhood training programmes at colleges and universities promote integrated working and some actually 'model' integrated working in the way they teach and support students. What they ask practitioners to do is to liaise with other early years settings, safeguard children's welfare, develop integrated interprofessional assessment and engage in training that underpins the importance of integrated working. However, this tells only half the story. Practitioners are not just expected to implement policies, they are required to lead and manage process on the ground. This means understanding and translating these expectations into actions that can be understood at a local level. It requires the ability to respond and understand duties associated with regulation and inspection, which includes providing evidence of integrated practice. It means having a clear idea of who to work with and forging ways of making this happen. It also means understanding the professional landscape, because this has changed and continues to evolve. It is now filled with many agencies and individuals who play a part in supporting families. These include:

- health visitors

- nurses

- family support workers

- doctors

- social workers

- police services

- teachers and schools

- administrators

- local authority officers

- quality improvement consultants

- local authority development workers

- pre- and after-school settings

- childminders

- other early years settings

- children's centres

- education services

- the voluntary sector.

Within this generic list of 'agencies' or 'professional groups' we find specialist professionals, such as those supporting speech and language, and in particular voluntary or 'third sector' groups active in the community. This could range from internet-based information networks, a local toy library, play schemes or voluntary home visiting services, all supporting vulnerable families and children. Practitioners are expected to share information with these agencies and those who work within them, which means having to learn any number of 'professional languages' in order to communicate effectively and keep in mind the needs of families and children. These we might call the 'new integrated practitioners'; they are refining practice, policies and procedures and changing the way we view integrated working. These practitioners are confident, capable and consistent in their approach to working with others and are part of a process of 'professionalisation', which is considered by a number of authors in Miller and Cable (2011). They become adept at managing change and develop the ability to shed preconceived ideas, to take on new roles and reflect on practice.

Indeed, many practitioners today have little experience of a professional life without change. This has meant re-evaluating their own role and the roles of others. For example, the *Common Core of Skills and Knowledge*, which sets out the expectations for integrated working on the role of practitioners and volunteers, states:

> As multi-agency working becomes more widely practised, it is increasingly referred to as integrated working, defined as where everyone supporting children, young people and families works together effectively, putting children, young people and their families at the centre of decision making in order to meet their needs and improve their lives. Practitioners should have the confidence to challenge situations by looking beyond your immediate role and asking considered questions . . . be assertive about what is required to avoid or remedy poor outcomes for the child or young person. (CWDC, 2010: 18)

This highlights the importance of putting the child, not professionals, at the centre of what goes on and the need for practitioners to have the confidence, skills and reflective abilities to challenge and assert themselves when involved with professional partners. Consequently, practitioners in a supervisory role are important and they are identified in the *2009 Childcare and Early Years Providers Survey* (Phillips et al., 2010) as the largest and fastest growing staff group in all types of childcare in the past four to seven years. It is therefore clear that leadership is important in terms of promoting integrated working, responding to change and coordinating a range of services that are now available to parents and families. Atkinson et al. (2007) found that this role could be seen as good practice in itself, and cite research by Harker et al. (2004), who found that it was also an important component in supporting inter-agency provision for young people with challenging behaviour. Likewise, Bagley et al. (2004) found that it was important to have a management structure that resided with mutual respect for others in a team. As to whether this helps us understand some of the inevitable status differences between early years practitioners and other professional groups, is a point for debate and yet to be resolved (EYSG, 2008).

Terminology, labels and forms of practice

There appear to be differences of interpretation when attempting to explain forms of inter-agency working, and a wide range of descriptors seem to be employed. For example, terminology includes the following: joined-up working, joint working, multi-agency, cross-agency working, multi-professional, multi-disciplinary working, cross-boundary working, collaborative, cooperative, coordinated and partnership working. To these might be added co-locational or core-located services, as well as specialist support workers and, increasingly, online coordinated support. They all mean different things and some are more local than others in the way they have evolved and developed. Unfortunately this tends to reinforce a professional landscape where practitioners see each other as having particular territories, titles and domains or 'levels of expertise'. The labelling terminology purports to indicate that services work together, but having such diverse descriptions can inhibit the very thing that they were intended to promote: to place the child and the family at the centre of practice, or what Carla Solvason, in Chapter 11, sees as the ability to share differing skills and understandings to work together towards the best outcome for children and families. We therefore need to do more than describe functions that may occur when people work together, and recognise that there must be a genuine desire to change working practices (Reed, 2010).

There is also a need to move away from a reliance on past definitions and practices. Rapid digital communication, databases and information exchange are making practitioners act and react differently. We need to look at our own professional landscapes of practice and consider carefully how we can collectively navigate our way towards a more informed way of working (Wenger et al., 2002; Warmington et al., 2004; Wenger, 2010), one that relies upon working within communities or teams, some performing specialist services, but all involved in sharing expertise. This means recognising the value and status of those who have striven to gain qualifications, such as a Foundation Degree, or further professional development such as the Early Years Professional Status in England (EYSG, 2008). All involve training that develops models of leadership as part of teamwork and the need to see collective professional synergy as important.

Does integrated working make a difference?

Atkinson et al. (2007) undertook a review of existing research and evaluation to explore different models of multi-agency work. They considered the impact, possible facilitators and challenges as well as the implications this had for good practice. They reported that in terms of the impact of multi-agency working there was an improvement to services and an increased understanding and trust between agencies. Relationships improved, as did communication, but there were some conflicting messages about whether multi-agency working resulted in an increased or reduced workload for the professionals involved. As for direct evidence of the impact on families, this was sparse. However, when there was collaboration there appeared to be a greater focus on preventing problems occurring with earlier referral and intervention. There was also a report exploring costs and outcomes of inter-agency training for safeguarding children (Carpenter et al., 2010). This comprehensive report revealed that although inter-agency training was mandated by government, participation was varied. There were concerns about the low participation of some professions taking the opportunity to attend specialist courses to update their knowledge and skills. There were, however, substantial and significant gains in knowledge and self-confidence regarding safeguarding policies and procedures and the opportunity to learn together was valued. Importantly, it suggested that government relies on the goodwill of professional and personal relationships to make this happen. This once again reminds us about the important role of early years service providers and the volume of time and energy they give to their role.

So is inter-agency, inter-professional or partnership working seen as valuable? The short answer appears to be 'yes', and importantly in ways that are of benefit to professionals, children and families. Conversely, there is evidence that when we do not work together there can be tragic consequences. Claire Majella Richards in Chapter 8 confronts this issue and explains the need for continued vigilance and the importance of working together in order to protect children. Percy-Smith (2005, 2006) also argues that partnership working is indeed valuable and again raises the point that it provides a collective energy that might not exist when we act alone. However, there needs to be care about not blurring roles and clear levels of expectation between different agencies and professionals. Gasper (2010) provides a comprehensive view of partnership working, stressing its worth and the detailed report *Evaluating the Early Impact of Integrated Children's Services* (Lord et al., 2008) suggests that parents and carers value a number of elements of integrated services, such as early identification and intervention and easier access to services. They found that parents recognise the value of joined-up inter-agency activity and that listening to parents' views was an important attribute for all professionals. McInnes (2007) suggests that communicating effectively can lead to positive benefits when agencies and individuals share information and expertise. All of which requires confidence on the part of the individual practitioner, as well as training, preferably with other disciplines, so that all play a part in the process and become advocates for families (Richards, 2010).

Integrated working requires the ability to demonstrate certain professional qualities (Messenger, 2010). Messenger attempts to draw together not only the perceived benefits of partnership working but the qualities necessary to engage in integrated working. She sees this as the relationship between knowledge and skills and makes a case that quality can be enhanced by professionals becoming aware of the relationships between each other and how these are formed and maintained. This requires an inside knowledge of day-to-day practice, and to an extent what Daniels et al. (2007: 535) describes as forms of 'rule-bending' and the creation of an organisational climate that 'supports flexible, responsive action' where professional identity is part of the process. There is also evidence from the work of Siraj-Blatchford and Siraj-Blatchford (2009) who explore ways of improving development outcomes for children through effective practice in integrating early years services. They found little definitive evidence on the impact of integrating services, but there was some indirect evidence to indicate that service integration may have a positive impact on outcomes. They suggest that further research is required. However, they make one particularly important point: that it is the *quality* rather than the *type* of integration that matters in terms of improving outcomes for children. Therefore, integrated working should be seen as more than a type of working, or identifying different ways of working; it is about placing the child at the centre, sharing information, and having a value system that sees integrated working as important and stops maintaining professional hierarchies at the expense of safeguarding children.

Aspects of practice seen as valuable within a quality improvement framework such as NQIN (2007) suggest that early years settings need support with developing inter-agency systems and information sharing. It infers a need for those with influence, such as development officers and quality improvement consultants, to communicate clear messages on the rationale and benefits of integrated working. However, we must remember that one factor alone is unlikely to move forward changes in attitudes or practice on the ground, but taken together and seen as part of an integrated policy framework these factors are highly important. This means that we are moving forward, perhaps not as quickly as we might, but communities of integrated practice are developing.

Quality integrated working

We accept that integrated working is a powerful part of developing quality in the early years. We accept that it is difficult to define and what we have is the product of centrally derived policy directives from government, assemblies and parliaments. It forms part of the safeguarding and protection of children and there is evidence that it provides speedier and more focused access to support. It is accepted that leadership is important in order to make things happen on the ground. However, we also accept that the impact of integrated working is varied and making it work is difficult, especially within a complex and changing landscape of professional practice. We realise that it is the quality of provision that matters, so what does 'quality integrated practice' look like? It is here that the real debate starts. We would like to think of it as a landscape where there is clearly a desire among practitioners to move towards integrated working (Warmington et al., 2004; Fitzgerald and Kay, 2008), a desire that may be driven by the factors and expectations we have described and one that should permeate all professional groups who touch children's lives. Within a changing professional landscape some of these may work under one roof or work locally and regionally sharing information. They may be easy to contact, they may be easy to talk to, they may have a positive and responsive view of working with others – and they may not. A practitioner, leader or supervisor must therefore deal with differing professional viewpoints and perspectives as well as professional hierarchies, structures and practices. They have to consider work cultures including their own 'stereotypes' of what other practitioners look like, and overcome a lack of trust: factors that we know hinder progress (Fitzgerald and Kay, 2008).

Recognising and dealing with trust is important, and this issue is a consequence of a long history of organisations not working together, not sharing information and having very different internal organisational polices. To this we could add insufficient funds, ring-fenced budgets, complex geographical boundaries, lack of time, multiple initiatives/targets, and problems in recruiting and retaining staff as other real issues hampering integrated work. This is not to be pessimistic or give up on the notion of what 'integrated quality' looks like. It is only to recognise that organisational difficulties, different forms of leadership and different organisational cultures often dominate our professional landscape. Therefore, quality must be dependent on understanding the different complexities involved and a consideration of what personal and professional dispositions it is possible to bring to bear. We contend that foremost of these is 'investing' time and trust in others (Warmington et al., 2004; Digman and Soan, 2008; Bachman et al., 2006). It also means developing the qualities necessary to engage in integrated working. Hence we place the word 'investing' in inverted commas, because forging integrated working requires an investment, and just like the warnings given to financial products, the value of an investment over time may go up or down. This means constantly monitoring and reflecting upon the way things are done and especially the impact upon children and families. The aim is to find a point where the process of improving quality through evaluation and reflection intersects with developing positive practice and action in the community.

Reflecting on a picture of professional practice

To imagine a positive way forward we need to look carefully at what we shall call the 'professional landscape' (Wenger, 2010). So let's imagine your landscape of practice, it may be flat, it may be mountainous, it may be swathed in mist, or it may be a landscape where everything is clear. Many professionals may sit, walk and wander around this landscape, and from a distance this may look as though they are working well together. For example, a children's centre may have multi-professional teams sharing the same space; there are various teams all under one roof. At first glance it may appear that integrated working has been achieved. However, on closer examination this landscape may in reality not be what is first expected. It could represent integrated working because a range of practitioners are co-located in one place, but this may result in 'parallel working', with little real attempt to jointly solve problems and where the old tradition of 'referring on' remains. It is therefore easy to make the presumption that professionals are prepared to cross difficult terrain; but we have to remember that some have differing professional viewpoints, differing structures, practices and work cultures.

In addition, power imbalances, professional hierarchies and different tribes may inhabit the landscape and it is rare for these to be easily negotiated. However, it is also true that one practice in the landscape may influence and inform another (Wenger, 2010). This is illustrated by Carla Solvason in Chapter 11 when she describes the way 'a team around the student' was created within a changing and diverse landscape of practice. Students were supported in a way that modelled good integrated working and this shows us the importance of acknowledging differences and understanding them. This can help develop an honest mutual respect, shared philosophies, and a common identity and agreed working principles. By understanding the landscape, it then becomes less problematic to move around, because with open dialogue and honesty comes an acceptance of the real issues that exist. All of this means a consideration of leading and changing practice.

Simkins (2005) sees this as three strands of enquiry, where practitioners reflect upon, first, *knowledge-for-practice*. This approach applies research and policy in practice, but also assumes that other professionals know what works well and that there is an established standard of best practice. It may therefore be necessary to ask challenging questions about why good practice is seen as good practice and what difference this makes to children and families. Second, practitioners need to reflect on *knowledge-in-practice*, which explores individual ways of working. This is an important strand of enquiry because practitioners need to have ownership and be inside their own practice where they can carefully reflect on what works best for them and what they would like to improve. Finally, *knowledge-of-practice* is where practitioners consider their work and place this within a wider social, cultural and political context and challenge ideas about leadership, power and influence.

Thinking in this way celebrates what we do well and identifies the factors that inhibit integrated working. We therefore agree with Karen Appleby and Mandy Andrews, in Chapter 4, that reflective practice is a vital tool to aid quality and is becoming increasingly recognised as important. This view is supported by Canavan et al. (2009), who explored policy developments in Ireland and found that reflective practice assists those engaging with theoretical and practical challenges of integrated working. In Wales, self-evaluation is seen as bringing about change and improvement using professional reflection, although in a minority of settings it had little impact on improving quality (EYSTN, 2010). This makes us think about whether such evaluation is effective when distanced from other support mechanisms. However, these are contemporary developments where change takes time and it is important to note that in Wales self-evaluation is seen as a starting point for all inspections, with settings encouraged to evaluate their own performance and ask questions about staff involvement in professional learning communities within and beyond the setting. Moreover, self-evaluation guidance looks outside Wales and itself develops reflection by leading practitioners towards examples of evaluative tools from other countries.

In England, Ofsted (2009) found that childminders who demonstrate outstanding practice see reflective practice as crucial to their success and regularly review what they do and how this helps children. This builds upon the National Strategies (2009: 19) report, *Progress Matters*, which states 'through continually reflecting on what the setting does well and what can be improved, a leader is able to instigate purposeful change'. The EYFS Practice Guidance (DCSF, 2008: 6/9) asks practitioners to 'lead and encourage a culture of reflective practice [where] practitioners should work together with professionals from other agencies'. In essence, this means realising that integrated working is based on the belief that we should work together so that all children fulfil their potential and we ensure that every child has the right to be protected. The failure of integrated communication, highlighted by serious case reviews, tells us how important communication is and shows how a regulatory process is in itself not enough (PSCB, 2010). Equally, it can be argued that the process of reflection in itself is not sufficient because it can sometimes reinforce rhetoric and make us feel that we are working together, just because we consider ways of working together. Perhaps a way forward is to return to the notion of professional synergy, as well as using and developing all the driving forces we have already discussed. This means practitioners working together, where the sum of their talents is greater than the parts. When regulation, inspection, local quality improvement support, reflective practice, integrated training, perceptive leadership and an understanding of local landscapes of practice are all in place, the likelihood of enhancing integrated quality is increased.

☐ Summary

In this chapter we have not shied away from the realisation that bringing together a broad range of disciplines is difficult. However, there are grounds for optimism in that there is today an acceptance that integrated working is important. This has been driven by a variety of actions, but still rests with practitioners to make it work. It certainly seems that integrated working makes a difference to families and children. It also makes a difference to the way practitioners work. As to whether this reduces or increases workload is still unclear. Of course, to make it work requires leadership that sees quality improvement as part of the process, alongside reflection, self-evaluation and the ability to challenge practice. This allows us to move away from looking at types of integrated practice and focus on the quality of practice. Importantly, integrated working is not a constant that can be represented by a description or captured on a diagram; it needs to change as the needs of families and children change. We therefore need to move away from thinking who controls what, to sharing who knows what. Finally, and essentially, practitioners are the glue that holds together integrated working. It is not an entity on its own and cannot be ordered up and served to parents and children. It relies on sustained reflection on practice.

References

Atkinson, M., Lamont, E. and Jones, M. (2007) *Multiagency Working and its Implication for Practice: A Review of the Literature.* Reading: CfBT Education Trust.

Bachman, M., Husbands, C. and O'Brien, M. (2006) *National Evaluation of the Children's Trusts: Managing Change.* Norwich: University of East Anglia and the National Children's Bureau.

Bagley, C., Ackerley, C. and Ratray, J. (2004) 'Social exclusion, Sure Start and organizational social capital: evaluating inter-disciplinary multi-agency working in an education and health work programme – documents and debates', *Journal of Education Policy,* 19 (5): 595–607.

Canavan, J., Coen, L., Dolan. and Whyte, L. (2009) 'Privileging practice: facing the challenge of integrated working for outcomes for children', *Children and Society,* 23 (5): 377–88.

Carpenter, J., Hackett, S., Patsios, D. and Szilassy, E. (2010) *Outcomes of Interagency Training to Safeguard Children: Final Report to the Department for Children, Schools and Families and the Department of Health.* Nottingham: DCSF and University of Bristol.

Children's Workforce Development Council (CWDC) (2007) *Common Assessment Framework for Children and Young People: Practitioners Guide.* Leeds: CWDC.

Children's Workforce Development Council (CWDC) (2010) *The Common Core of Skills and Knowledge*. Leeds: CWDC.

Daniels, H., Leadbetter, J., Warmington, P., Edwards, A., Martin, D., Popova, A., Apostolov, A., Middleton, D. and Brown, S. (2007) 'Learning in and for multi-agency working', *Oxford Review of Education*, 33 (4): 521–38.

Department for Children, Schools and Families (DCSF) (2008) *Practice Guidance for the Early Years Foundation Stage*. Nottingham: DCSF.

Digman, C. and Soan, S. (2008) *Working with Parents – A Guide for Educational Professionals*. London: Sage.

Early Years Stakeholders Group (EYSG) (2008) *Report to the Children's Minister*. Available at: http://www.teachernet.gov.uk/_doc/13256/Early_Years_Stakeholder_Report_FINAL2.doc (last accessed 22 December 2010).

EYSTN (2010) *Self-evaluation for Non-maintained Settings*. Cardiff: Her Majesty's Inspectorate for Education and Training in Wales.

Fitzgerald, D. and Kay, J. (2008) *Working Together in Children's Services*. Abingdon: David Fulton.

Gasper, M. (2010) *Multi-agency Working in the Early Years*. London: Sage.

Lord, P., Kinder, K., Wilkin, A., Atkinson, M. and Harland, J. (2008) *Evaluating the Early Impact of Integrated Children's Services: Round 1 Final Report*. Slough: NFER.

McInnes, K. (2007) *A Practitioner's Guide to Interagency Working in Children's Centres: A Review of the Literature*. London: Barnardo's Policy and Research Unit.

Messenger, W. (2010) 'Managing multi-agency working', in M. Reed and N. Canning (eds), *Reflective Practice in the Early Years*. London: Sage.

Miller, L. and Cable, C. (2011) *Professionalization, Leadership and Management in the Early Years*. London: Sage.

National Quality Improvement Network (NQIN) (2007) *Quality Improvement Principles: A Framework for Local Authorities and National Organisations to Improve Quality Outcomes for Children and Young People*. London: National Children's Bureau.

National Strategies (2009) *Progress Matters: Reviewing and Enhancing Young Children's Development*. Nottingham: DCSF.

Office for Standards in Education (Ofsted) (2009) *Childminding: A Passion to be Outstanding*. Manchester: Crown Copyright.

Percy-Smith, J. (2005) *Definitions and Models: What Works in Strategic Partnerships for Children*. London: Barnardo's Policy and Research Unit.

Percy-Smith, J. (2006) 'What works in strategic partnerships for children: a research review', *Children and Society*, 20 (4): 313–23.

Phillips, R., Norden, O., McGinigal, S., Garnett, E. and Oseman, D. (2010) *2009 Childcare and Early Years Providers Survey*, Research Brief DFE-RB012. London: Department for Education.

Plymouth Safeguarding Children's Board (PSCB) (2010) *Serious Case Review Overview Report Executive Summary in respect of Nursery Z*. Plymouth: Safeguarding Children's Board. Available at: http://www.plymouth.gov.uk/serious_case_review_nursery_z.pdf (last accessed 22 December 2010).

Reed, M. (2010) 'Children's centres and children's services?', in M. Reed and N. Canning (eds), *Reflective Practice in the Early Years*, London: Sage.

Reed, M., and Canning, N. (2009) 'Curriculum diversity for early years in the four nations of the United Kingdom', conference paper, *European Early Childhood Education Research Association 19th Conference*, Strasbourg, August.

Richards, C.M. (2010) 'Safeguarding children: Every Child Matters so everybody matters!', in M. Reed and N. Canning (eds), *Reflective Practice in the Early Years*. London: Sage.

Simkins, T. (2005) 'Leadership in education: "what works" or "what makes sense"?', *Educational Management Administration and Leadership*, 33 (1): 9–26.

Siraj-Blatchford, I. and Siraj-Blatchford, J. (2009) *Improving Development Outcomes for Children Through Effective Practice in Integrating Early Years Services*. London: Centre for Excellence and Outcomes in Children and Young People's Services (C4EO).

Warmington, P., Daniels, H., Edwards, A., Brown, S., Leadbetter, J., Martin, D. and Middleton, D. (2004) *Interagency Collaboration: A Review of the Literature*. Bath: Teaching and Learning Research Council – Learning in and for Interagency Working Project.

Wenger, E. (2010) 'Landscapes of Practice', a series of workshops held at the Practice-based Professional Learning Centre for Excellence in Teaching and Learning. Milton Keynes: Open University.

Wenger, E., McDermott, R. and Snyder, W. (2002) *Cultivating Communities of Practice*. Cambridge, MA: Harvard Business School Press.

4

Reflective practice is the key to quality improvement

Karen Appleby and Mandy Andrews

Chapter overview

This chapter explores reflective practice in relation to quality improvement. We argue that the process of improving quality is best served by practitioners who apply key principles of reflective practice but also have the capacity to consider and understand their own reflective activity. This perspective has a value base that champions the role of individuals in effecting change and improvement. Reflective practice is explained and considered as a complex, multi-faceted process which in its most effective form is personalised and owned by practitioners. We argue against seeing reflective practice as an externally acquired or applied model of thinking and action, preferring to consider it as a personalised 'way of being' that values individual professional identity and qualities. A 'weave' of practice is central to this chapter, which represents complex interrelationships between professional qualities and the external influences for quality improvement and change. The 'weave' is presented and explained as both an illustration and a way of supporting reflexive self-awareness, understanding and ownership of the reflective process. Attention is also given to the potential of intuitive, creative and playful ways of being and the relevance of reflective collaboration with others.

Quality improvement and the role of the individual

We view quality improvement as an ongoing process that is supported by external standards or frameworks rather than being driven by them. We could see quality as a 'checklist' of performance but this would be contrary to our belief in the agency of individuals and their potential for 'creating possibilities rather than pursuing predefined goals' (Fortunati, 2006: 37). Individual potential is further supported by Brooker and Edwards (2010), who argue for a move towards a culture that nurtures an individual's capacity to act as a free and thoughtful agent with a commitment to improving his or her world. In a context where 'quality' is perceived as being assessed by external forces, practitioners can sometimes find it difficult to stand up for what they value and to act as 'free agents'. This perceived lack of freedom can lead to a feeling of disempowerment, which can translate into a negative effect on commitment to quality improvement and change.

Table 4.1 Defining reflective practice

Terminology	Description
Reflective practice	A practitioner's personal engagement with reflective activity. This activity is perceived as a 'way of being' which includes: • reflective thinking/reflection (both cognitive and affective) • reflective learning • reflective action
Reflective thinking/ reflection	Includes self-aware, creative and critical thinking informed by evidence. It involves both *reflection* (holding the mirror up to the world: seeing things from a new perspective) and *reflexivity* (holding up the mirror to self: questioning oneself to gain greater personal awareness and understanding)
Cognitive activities	Logical successive thinking processes
Affective activities	Actions taken to understand emotions and emotional responses
Reflective learning	Insight gained from reflective thinking
Reflective action	The act of applying what has been learnt through reflective thinking

It is possible, however, for practitioners to act as a 'thoughtful agents' within a framework of professional situations, even when those situations are triggered by external forces. This involves creating the opportunity, space and time needed to think about practice and the appropriate action emerging from a reflective thinking process. We argue that being a 'thoughtful agent' also requires a deeper understanding of self and of the nature of personal engagement with ongoing reflective activity. This approach enables practitioners to question the 'paradigms in which one is operating' (Peeters and Vandenbroeck, 2011: 63) and to be responsive to the need for change and quality improvement in relation to the specific needs of children, families and settings. Consequently, it requires an understanding of what we mean by being a reflective practitioner, including understanding the terminology we use and the interpretation we apply throughout this chapter. Table 4.1 explains how we use the terminology that surrounds reflective practice in this chapter.

Reflective practice

Reflective practice has been identified by educators as beneficial for quality improvement (Argyris and Schon, 1978; Boud et al., 1985; Brookfield, 1987; Brockbank and McGill, 2007). It has been described as a generic term for 'those intellectual and affective activities in which individuals engage to explore their experiences in order to lead to new understandings and appreciation' (Boud et al., 1985: 19). In addition, reflection has the capacity to create 'alternative and more productive ways of organising the workplace' (Brookfield, 1987: 14). Together these two statements indicate that examining our actions and activities, both at a cognitive and an emotional level, can help practitioners to think and learn from experience in order to improve practice. Such reflective activity can also be creative, offering different, new and more effective ways of organising things, whether applied when working with children or colleagues or to the way we organise the environment. Expressed simply, the core principles of reflective practice involve reflective thinking and learning, which are used to inform decisions and actions in practice, and by implication, improve quality.

A number of 'models' have evolved to support reflective thinking and practice. Many of these, such as Kolb's (1984) model of experiential learning, Ghaye and Ghaye's (1998) 'reflection-on-practice' and Brookfield's (1995) 'lenses', have the clear purpose of supporting critical thinking about experience and using what is learnt from this process to inform future actions. In addition Ghaye (2011: 28) draws on the work of Baumeister (1991) and asks us to see reflection as a meaning-making process that includes the satisfaction of 'four personal needs of purpose, value, efficacy and self-worth'. However, while many recognise the role of self-reflection and the influence of a range of personal 'drivers', they do not necessarily encourage practitioners to understand, take ownership or utilise the unique nature of their reflective activity. Ownership draws on a range of personal factors, such as heritage, disposition, skills and understanding. A deeper level of engagement with reflective activity also requires understanding and appreciation of personal potential. Self-awareness can support reflective practice that is personally meaningful and therefore more likely to produce the energy and drive necessary to make significant differences in terms of quality. This perspective includes recognition and acceptance of unique ways of being reflective and how this is supported by an individual's specific professional qualities. Such an approach values different ways of engaging with reflective activity and professes no single model or particular professional context. It also supports the development of reflexive practitioners who question 'taken for granted beliefs' and develop an 'understanding that knowledge is contestable' (Peeters and Vanderbroeck, 2011: 63). Peeters and Vanderbroeck argue that such reflexivity supports a focus on 'doing the right things rather than doing things right', a key principle that we believe underpins the process of improving quality.

An individual's reflective activity often takes place within a dynamic and changeable socio-cultural context, which shapes the processes, responses and individuals involved. While the core values and principles of an individual may remain constant and be articulated and understood as a basis for reflective activity, there are many ways of responding to issues according to context. Developing as a reflective practitioner means being someone who is able to act in ways that make a qualitative difference and it requires an understanding of the current socio-cultural context and how this affects the nature of professional responses. Bronfenbrenner's (1986) ecological model may help us to explore this concept of socio-cultural influence on reflective identity and practice. According to Bronfenbrenner an individual's development is affected by a series of environmental influences: the 'microsystem' of family, school, or neighbourhood; the 'exosystem' of a town, local policy, or economic influences; and the 'macrosystem' of cultural influences, national policy, or pervading ideology. A practitioner's reflective practice may likewise be influenced by colleagues, peers, managers and parents at a setting; who in turn may be influenced by local quality improvement policy, risk awareness, and economic status; and overall this is influenced by central government policy and perhaps the perceived 'culture' of the type of setting.

Therefore practitioners may subtly shift in perceived identity and consequent reflective responses according to the social and environmental situation in which they find themselves. The ability to engage positively and constructively within a changing professional landscape is supported by an individual's understanding of both that landscape and what is possible within a particular situation in terms of their personal responses and qualities. Just as external socio-cultural spheres influence responses, the reflective activity by an individual may influence future quality improvement in others because the practitioner is an 'active' agent within their professional context. Recognising and valuing the impact of this agency may offer an opportunity for reflective practice to be a 'means of empowerment, leading to change at the individual and societal level' (Cable and Miller, 2008: 173). Developing a strong sense of one's own identity as a reflective practitioner can have a significant impact on both individual and collective confidence to engage in reflective activity as a means of improving quality.

Reflective practice as a 'way of being'

Understanding reflective practice as a 'way of being' that is owned and experienced by a practitioner encourages the development of an individual as a 'reflective professional practitioner rather than as a technician' (Moss, 2008: xiii). This allows for the identification of different ways of engaging within a process. A 'technician' may go through the motions of making changes in practice by following a prescribed model of reflective practice. However, it is essential for a 'reflective professional practitioner' to emotionally and intellectually 'own' the process (Moss, 2008: xiii). Ownership means acknowledging that reflective practice can include the use of deeply embedded intuitive 'reflex responses' and 'ways of knowing' (Atkinson and Claxton, 2000: 2). Atkinson and Claxton argue that we should value 'other forms of reflection' that do not focus solely on reason and articulation; rather, 'unconscious insight draws on the whole of what has been known'; the enormity and complexity of which cannot always be articulated (2000: 5). Encouraging practitioners to use their full range of personal resources within reflective activity is essential. It is possible that compliance with a prescribed 'model' limits reflective potential by indicating one preferred way of proceeding towards reflection, or even towards quality improvement. We would suggest that without alternatives, such reliance on an external 'expert' model may leave practitioners feeling de-skilled and disempowered. Recognition of reflective practice as unique to individuals celebrates difference, recognises personal development and is therefore inclusive.

Enabling practitioners to utilise their full range of personal resources within reflective activity requires a critical view of what is involved. There is a view that intuitive forms of knowledge and 'ways of knowing' have been unjustly ignored in our rational technical world (Atkinson and Claxton, 2000). For Atkinson and Claxton intuitive and 'tacit' forms of knowledge in practice are of equal value and should be equally validated and respected. They even argue that there are times when we can 'think too much' in rationalising processes when we should rely on a more instinctive way of being. This suggests that there is a form of professional reflection that is much more intuitive and instinctive and relies on the inner resources of a practitioner. We see this as important in the context of developing early years practice, which requires an understanding of many complex issues. Kreiner and Sheep (2010) suggest that reflective intuition should be respected as a 'way of knowing' that is particularly useful in dealing with complexity. Intuitive reflective practice respects and releases inner qualities and understandings, which inform actions taken to improve quality in practice.

Many models of reflective practice represent what seems to be a relatively simple process. Investigation into the nature of a practitioner's 'real life' participation in reflective practice reveals a complex array of professional qualities applied and synthesised in different ways at different times according to the situation. Understanding the coming together of the individual and context offers a way of understanding reflective activity from a deeply personal perspective. Through a process of making 'human sense' (Donaldson, 1987) of one's own reflective activity, practitioners can evaluate the ways and extent to which they make changes for the better in all aspects of life. Personalised reflective activity that becomes a positive experience and rewards aspects of self is more likely to become a disposition or 'habit of mind' (Arnold, 2003), owned by the individual. Practitioners who understand the nature of their own engagement in reflective practice are more likely to be emotionally as well as intellectually involved in the process.

Reflective activity: a complex weave

In seeking to understand personalised reflective activity it is necessary to return to the core principles of reflective practice identified earlier in this chapter; that is, reflective thinking and learning that is used to inform decisions and actions in practice. We have argued that awareness and understanding of self as reflective practitioners within a socio-cultural context strengthens an individual's potential for improving quality through this process. Figure 4.1 illustrates a 'weave' of how an individual might engage with reflective activity within the context of professional situations. Reflective activity is very specific to individual and professional contexts and therefore engaging with reflective activity creates a 'woven mat' that illustrates a specific narrative or 'story' within the context of professional practice at any one time. The weave can be used as a way of understanding the nature of reflective activity in a theoretical sense but it also has potential as a tool for recognising, valuing and developing individual reflective activity.

Figure 4.1 represents reflective activity as a weave of different professional qualities that may be drawn upon in relation to a variety of professional concerns and areas for quality improvement. The horizontal threads, representing potential qualities, interweave with the vertical threads, representing external factors. It is not possible to represent the 'authentic lived activity' (Brookfield, 1987) of any one individual, but the diagram offers an opportunity to explore the specific nature of personal reflective activity in context. The weave should not, therefore, be seen as a series of separate aspects of practice. The different threads of personal qualities and stimuli from external factors all interrelate and weave together to create the 'woven mat' of reflective activity. The horizontal threads offer a number of prompts for analysing the nature of personal reflective activity. They are aspects of who you are as a person and practitioner; they are qualities that support the ability to improve quality through reflective practice. These qualities underpin the 'action-oriented competencies' that create the possibility for changing practice (Peeters and Vanderbroeck, 2011: 70). Use of the threads as prompts may inform critical self-awareness, gradually developing into a 'woven mat' of self-knowledge and in turn supporting the development of professional identity. The reflexive practitioner seeks to acknowledge and question who they are, asking: What am I like? What are my particular preferred ways of being, skills and characteristics? Do I generate creativity and risk-taking behaviours? Am I brave enough to generate and take new risks for improvement? These are what Ghaye (2011: 35) describes as

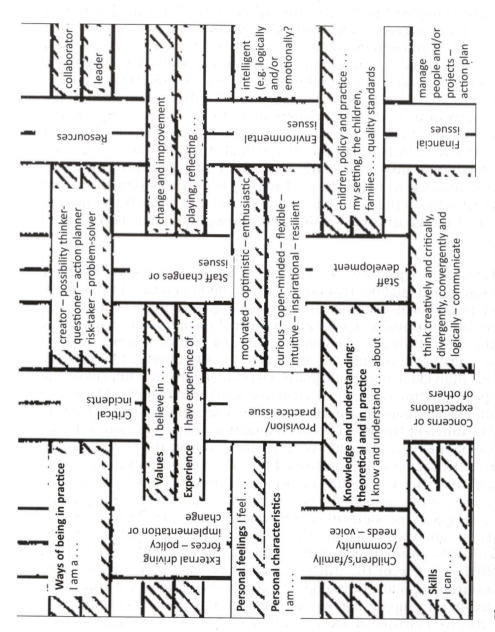

Figure 4.1 Weave of professional qualities and external factors

'positive questions'. He focuses on reflective learning supported by 'why-type' and 'how-type' questions; we would add 'who am I-type' and 'what am I-type' questions.

How we behave at any particular time is often only so in relation to the context and relationships we have with others (Ragins, 2010). The vertical threads identify potential external factors or influences on reflective practitioners and their efforts to improve quality. There are many triggers for quality improvement, which are often both stimulating and limiting. Resources are one such example; while a new children's centre may have a range of new but poorly utilised play equipment, a local community nursery with limited funding may take greater risks by creating alternative and innovative play opportunities with cheaper, donated resources. As with any weave, adding more 'threads' increases the strength of the material, its resilience and durability as well as its potential for different uses in the future. Experience of developing and applying personal and professional qualities in relation to different challenges strengthens the weave and therefore the potential for improving quality through further reflective activity. Recognising, understanding and valuing these experiences can encourage reflective activity as a 'habit of mind' (Arnold, 2003) or 'way of being'. This awareness and understanding of self has the potential for empowering individuals as reflective practitioners through a process of personal change and improvement, as well as supporting quality improvement in practice through institutional change. It also has the potential for enabling a practitioner's engagement in current issues affecting the early years sector. The complex nature of reflective activity means that there are many possible threads to be identified. We have identified several of the qualities represented by the horizontal threads for further consideration. These different qualities, which include 'ways of being in practice', 'values and beliefs' and 'experiences', are closely related and are likely to impact on each other.

Ways of being in practice

'Ways of being in practice' are the roles practitioners assume when actively engaged in reflective practice. They are particularly significant when exploring the idea of identity as a reflective practitioner and the nature of reflective activity at different times and in different situations. For example, you may recognise yourself as the creator in a group, coming up with new ideas; you may be a person who asks how things will work, or how they can be implemented; or you may be the one who takes risks and encourages risk-taking in others. Practitioners should also consider how they are in relation to others: whether they are a collaborator, a leader, or a combination of both. The role of 'creator' as a way of being in practice is significant within reflective activity. Yelland et al. (2008) remind us that in the future there will be a premium desire for those citizens who are able to be creative, innovative and transformative in their use of knowledge and skills. They highlight the acquisition of new knowledge, but also the ability to make connections with existing knowledge, to analyse situations, and develop 'habits of learning'. Such skills enable individuals to be autonomous, flexible and able to 'adapt well to the changing circumstances that tend to define our contemporary lives' (2008: 4). This perspective informs an understanding of reflective practice as an evidence-based process reliant on knowledge and critical thinking, and also the need for practitioners who are 'reflexive and agentic subjects' (Peeters and Vandenbroeck, 2011: 64). Making a significant impact on the quality of practice requires the ability to create new possibilities in complex professional situations and for the practitioner to be what Craft (2008: 5) describes as a 'possibility thinker'. Being creative in practice reflects a view of creativity, supported by Kaufman et al. (2010) and Rosie Walker in Chapter 7, that we all have the potential to be creative.

Within the context of creative reflective practice we argue that practitioners should consider the relevance of being playful and how their role as a 'player' can facilitate new possibilities and therefore impact on quality. In common with the idea of being creative, the role of the player is not a 'way of being' that many would recognise in their own practice. Playful behaviour may be perceived as inappropriate for adults and particularly for professionals. We argue, however, that playful reflective activity should be recognised and valued because it is possible to 'create meaning, possibility and new insights through the processes of play' (Tracey, 2007: 3). From this perspective, playful reflection on experiences can open up new ways of understanding. Learning from this process can then inform ways of improving practice. However, we should also remember that we can be reflective without taking any action for improvement. It is the doing something 'in practice' or the action arising from our reflection that results in quality improvement through change. Adopting a playful approach to action planning as well as reflection can support practitioners in imagining different possibilities, evaluating potential outcomes and engaging in trial and error where appropriate. The concept of a 'playful reflective practitioner' includes the capacity to think intuitively, creatively, at speed and with energy: to be a 'simultaneous' thinker (Hall, 2007). In his writing about play, Hughes (2001) makes links between the creativity of play and what he calls 'combinatorial flexibility': the speed by which a number of diverse ideas come together to explore and inform an action or solution. He argues that an environment supportive of play, together with a 'playful disposition' encourages 'combinatorial flexibility'. The implication for reflective practitioners is that they need to be operating in a supportive context for this capacity or potential for playful reflective thinking to be realised. Some may argue that this is difficult or even impossible in practice, for any number of reasons, but perhaps we should be actively and positively considering how this can be achieved.

Values and beliefs

A practitioner's way of being in practice is likely to be informed by values and experiences. Values are those things we hold as central to ourselves and the actions we take, our 'enduring beliefs' (Avery, 2004: 102). Core values and beliefs are deeply held and likely to influence all that we do, whether by choice or subconsciously. Abbott and Langston (2005: 57) remind us that for professionals to work effectively with children and families 'their first duty is to recognise themselves for who they are, what they believe and why'. This same recognition is required for ownership and implementation of reflective practice and related approaches for quality improvement. A reflective practitioner may recognise that we are all shaped by our individual experiences from childhood onwards. Early and strong experiences influence our core values (Avery, 2004). For example, if your experience as a very young child was one of playing outdoors with individual freedom this is likely to be retained as a core value and applied in your work. However, these core values can sometimes hinder the process of quality improvement if reflective thinking and action are informed by emotional responses to the detriment of a more balanced approach that also considers logic and socio-cultural factors. A reflexive practitioner should be able to recognise when responses are subjective and affected by personal bias.

Experiences

Early and strong experiences not only influence individual values but can also shape the way a person's brain works and influence the connections they subsequently make (Hall, 2007). Hall describes two ways of taking on and processing information: 'successive processing' and 'simultaneous processing'. Successive processing is largely an applied learning process: the implementation of someone else's 'way of doing things' such as learning a skill, playing a musical instrument, or driving a car. Successive processing requires step-by-step thinking. In contrast, simultaneous processing draws together a range of data and influences and applies these at the same time and at speed (Hall, 2007). Similarly, reflective practice may be 'learnt' as a model or 'experienced' as a simultaneous thinking process. An experienced practitioner's approach will draw on their 'bank' of influential prior experiences, values, qualities and skills, but they may or may not be able to process this resource to best effect. Less experienced practitioners may have the capacity to process 'data' simultaneously but will not have the same resources from practice. These differences support an argument for recognising and valuing individual differences and developing strong collaborative working practices that utilise these to support reflective activity and therefore improve quality.

In addition to early life experiences, a person's early work experiences are likely to influence their professional selves as new skills and 'ways of being' in a particular context are retained. For example, a health-based worker will work very differently from a community development worker. As beneficial experiences become embedded they form a part of the 'way we think'. Awareness of the influence of individual experiences on a personal response is helpful in understanding personal reflective practice. Practitioners are then able simultaneously to draw on and process a range of aspects of self and external stimuli in response to prompts for improvement. The qualities that practitioners draw upon are not merely external 'models' or learnt ways of doing things, but include personal values and experiences, knowledge and skills practised so far.

Developing awareness and understanding of your identity

There are many prompts to improvement and many practitioner qualities, but there is also an art in applying both aspects in practice. Together the vertical and horizontal threads in Figure 4.1 form a weave that offers a model for increasing awareness of reflective self, while acknowledging the range of stimulants for purposeful reflective action in a professional context. The weave supports a reflexive awareness and understanding of self-identity in the context of practice and acknowledges individual strengths. A strong 'weave' of skills, qualities and understandings should be empowering when participating or leading quality reflective practice for improvement. For developing practitioners the weave offers a way of valuing a wide range of personal and professional qualities. The external factors will vary, dependent on roles and responsibilities but the potential for understanding, valuing and developing relevant qualities remains. Sometimes one quality held by an individual is stronger than others. With self-knowledge a practitioner will undertake reflective practice in their own way, with additional understanding of what that 'way' is and confidence in the purpose and value of the process.

The social dimension of reflective activity

The social dimension of reflective activity and quality improvement should not be underestimated. At any point in the reflective process, and depending on the focus, there is potential for colleagues, children and families to be involved in challenging and developing practice. Reflection with others involves 'co-constructing knowledge, making and sharing meaning' (Appleby, 2010: 19). Talking through our own perspectives or arguing our value-laden concepts of practice and quality helps to articulate our understanding. Reflection in dialogue with others not only considers the factors and resources that stimulate change, it also assists in articulating and 'reframing practice preventing stuck habits' that can sometimes stifle improvement (Brockbank and McGill, 2007: 143).

Paige-Smith and Craft (2008: 170–7) discuss Wenger's concept of a community of practice (1998) and its relevance for reflection and the development of practice. They suggest that the social processes involved in practice support participation in reflective thinking and meaning-making, and also have the potential to support collective endeavour. This endeavour is often focused on a shared interest driven by participants, rather than an 'external force' (Paige-Smith and Craft, 2008: 173). Individual differences and similarities, and the recognition of these in discussions, play an important part in developing the effectiveness of communities of practice. The benefits include the development of 'collaborative/shared perspectives' (2008: 174) which underpin effective developments in team practice. This collective perspective validates the emphasis on empowering reflective practitioners and nurturing ownership of the reflective process. A strong sense of identity, supported by self-knowledge, enables effective participation in a professional community and therefore the impact of that community on quality improvement.

Summary

In this chapter we have argued for personal engagement with critical reflective thinking and learning which, when applied to action, has the potential to generate change and improvement in practice. We have highlighted how ownership of the reflective process requires an understanding not only of experience but also of self and context. Too often the reflective process is seen as the technical application of a reflective model to prompt thinking on a situation or the environment. In contrast, our concept of reflective practice requires personal engagement and acknowledgement of self as part of a complex and multi-faceted process. It is underpinned by awareness of personal and professional qualities that create the possibility of change and improvement. These personal 'threads' provide a rich resource for reflective thinking, learning and action. Understanding personal engagement with reflective activity also requires recognition of how personal and professional qualities are applied within the context of external influences or 'threads'. The 'woven mat' created by a practitioner's reflective activity in context supports a personal awareness that offers self-efficacy and nurtures a reflective disposition. Reflective activity is therefore seen as a 'way of being' that emerges with time, experience and, essentially, self-knowledge. Quality improvement is best served by reflective practitioners who have the capacity to move beyond the basic principles of reflective practice. They need the opportunity and confidence to recognise and value their own reflective activity and the disposition and ability to engage in reflective activity with others. Reflective practice should involve a rigorous process of making sense of self and experience. The outcome of this process has the potential to inform and stimulate effective change and development in practice, leading to improvement in the quality of provision for children and their families.

References

Abbott, L. and Langston, A. (eds) (2005) *Birth to Three Matters: Supporting the Framework of Effective Practice*. Maidenhead: Open University Press.

Appleby, K. (2010) 'Reflective thinking, reflective practice', in M. Reed and N. Canning (eds), *Reflective Practice in the Early Years*. London: Sage.

Argyris, C. and Schon, D. (1978) *Organisational Learning*. Reading, MA: Addison Wesley.

Arnold, C. (2003) *Observing Harry: Child Development and Learning 2–5*. London: Sage.

Atkinson, T. and Claxton, G. (2000) 'Introduction', in T. Atkinson and G. Claxton (eds), *The Intuitive Practitioner: On the Value of Not Always Knowing What One is Doing*. Buckingham: Open University Press.

Avery, G.C. (2004) *Understanding Leadership: Paradigms and Cases*. London: Sage.

Boud, D., Keogh, R. and Walker, D. (1985) 'Promoting reflection in learning: a model', in D. Boud, R. Keogh and D. Walker (eds), *Reflection: Turning Experience into Learning*. London: Kogan Page.

Brockbank, A. and McGill, I. (2007) *Facilitating Reflective Learning in Higher Education*. Maidenhead: Open University Press.

Bronfenbrenner, U. (1986) 'Ecology of the family as a context for human development', *Developmental Psychology*, 22 (6): 723–42.

Brooker, L. and Edwards, S. (2010) 'Introduction: from challenging to engaging play', in L. Brooker, and S. Edwards (eds), *Engaging Play*. Maidenhead: Open University Press.

Brookfield, S. (1987) *Developing Critical Thinkers*. Maidenhead: Open University Press.

Brookfield, S. (1995) *Becoming a Critically Reflective Teacher*. San Francisco: Jossey-Bass.

Cable, C. and Miller, L. (2008) 'Looking to the future', in L. Miller and C. Cable (eds), *Professionalism in the Early Years*. London: Hodder Education.

Craft, A. (2008) 'Creativity in early years settings', in A. Paige-Smith and A. Craft (eds), *Developing Reflective Practice in the Early Years*, Maidenhead: Open University Press.

Donaldson, M. (1987) *Children's Minds*. London: Fontana.

Fortunati, A. (2006) *The Education of Young Children as a Community Project*. Italy: Edizioni Jnr SRL with Children in Scotland.

Ghaye, T. (2011) *Teaching and Learning Through Reflective Practice: A Practical Guide for Positive Action* (2nd edition). London: Routledge.

Ghaye, T. and Ghaye, K. (1998) *Teaching and Learning Through Critical Reflective Practice*. London: David Fulton Press.

Hall, N. (2007) 'Brain functioning: simultaneous and successive processing', conference paper, *17th Annual Conference of the European Teacher Education Network*, Portugal, April. Available at: http://www.eten-online.org/img/publications/ETEN%2017%20proceedings.pdf#page=96 (last accessed 13 January 2010).

Hughes, B. (2001) *Evolutionary Playwork and Reflective Analytic Practice*. London: Routledge.

Kaufman, J., Beghetto, R., Baer, J. and Ivcevic, Z. (2010) 'Creativity polymathy: what Benjamin Franklin can teach your kindergartener', *Learning and Individual Differences*, 20: 380–7.

Kolb, D. (1984) *Experiential Learning: Experience as the Source of Learning and Development*. London: Prentice-Hall.

Kreiner, G.E. and Sheep, M.L. (2010) 'Growing pains and gains: framing identity dynamics as opportunities for identity growth', in L. Morgan Roberts and J.E. Dutton (eds), *Exploring Positive Identities and Organisations*. London: Routledge.

Moss, P. (2008) 'Foreword', in A. Paige-Smith and A. Craft (eds), *Developing Reflective Practice in the Early Years* (2nd edition). Maidenhead: Open University Press.

Paige-Smith, A. and Craft, A. (2008) 'Reflection and developing a community of practice', in A. Paige-Smith and A. Craft (eds), *Developing Reflective Practice in the Early Years* (2nd edition). Maidenhead: Open University Press.

Peeters, J. and Vandenbroeck, M. (2011) 'Childcare practitioners and the process of professionalization', in L. Miller and C. Cable (eds), *Professionalization, Leadership and Management in the Early Years*. London: Sage.

Ragins, R. (2010) 'Positive identities in action: a model of mentoring self-structures and the motivation to mentor', in L. Morgan Roberts and J.E. Dutton (eds), *Exploring Positive Identities and Organizations*. London: Routledge.

Tracey, S. (2007) 'Creative reflection, creative practice: expressing the inexpressible', conference paper, Creativity or Conformity? Building Cultures of Creativity in Higher Education. University of Wales Institute and Higher Education Academy (HEA), Cardiff, 8–10 January.

Yelland, N., Lee, L., O'Rourke, M. and Harrison, C. (2008) *Rethinking Learning in Early Childhood Education*. Maidenhead: Open University Press.

Section 2

Quality Improvement in Action

5

Exploring the concept of quality play

Natalie Canning

Chapter overview

This chapter explores the relationship between developing quality
provision and children's play. They are important aspects of early
years practice which are both subjective and dependent upon
personal perspectives, values and beliefs. Exploring quality and
play in practice exposes a debate surrounding the construct
of play; as a process, or reliant on measurable outcomes.
It is interwoven within a wider debate about quality being
seen as achieving performance indicators to the detriment of
concentrating on the experiences of children. Essentially, quality
and play can be oriented to achieve an outcome; however, for
quality play to occur practitioners need to focus on how play
opportunities are cultivated within a setting. Consequently this
chapter explores quality principles for play which emerge
from a child-centred, free play perspective, recognising the
voice and autonomy of the child in play to support quality
experiences.

In this chapter a position or viewpoint is taken about children's
play in early years settings. Emphasis is given to the importance of
recognising the child's agenda, how sensitively observations of play
are interpreted and what the information is used for. The concept

of play advocated throughout comes from a particular perspective, underpinned by a view of play that is organised and self-motivated by individual or groups of children. Child-directed or child-centred play allows children a degree of freedom and the ability to personally direct what they are doing. They are afforded a sense of autonomy, controlling what they do, how they do it and when to stop or change their play. Hughes (2001) refers to this as 'free play'. However, there are inevitable restrictions on free play, such as the parameters of the environment, the type and scale of resources and the influence of practitioners. Kalliala (2006) argues that these factors influence how children play and the choices they make, and they also form the landscape of play the children engage in (Veale, 2001). The role of the practitioner is central to the way in which children are able to experience 'free play'. In providing a child-centred environment that recognises the significance of giving children time and space for free choice, practitioners can develop an informed understanding of children's unique qualities and their interests on which to base further learning opportunities.

Creating an ethos based on following children's ideas and motivations requires practitioners to trust children and value free play. Child-directed or free play can be unpredictable and giving children a voice means that someone has to listen, take on board what children say and be prepared to respond sensitively and appropriately. Consequently, practitioners who place free play at the centre of practice need to be flexible in their approach and facilitate a space that allows play to develop, and develop in a way that the child intends, while bearing in mind health and safety. Children know how to play and it usually carries a meaning for the child, for example revisiting something that has happened at home, rehearsing something they want to say or do, solving a problem, recreating a feeling, practising roles or working out a relationship (Hughes, 2001; Sutton Smith, 1997). The meaning in play is not always apparent to the onlooker and play can often be misinterpreted (without intention). The ability to see play through a child's eyes is a skill that requires experience and the ability to reflect on practice, as well as knowledge and understanding of the child's background, their personality and their individual needs. Therefore the wealth of insights into a child's individual qualities and experiences that play can generate should not be underestimated. Supporting children's free play requires careful consideration of the environment, children's individual needs, the relationships that are already established and those that emerge or develop through play. These considerations form the basis for recognising that children have a capacity for developing ways of seeing the world, problem-solving, learning and developing 'meaning-making' in their play.

Play is a term that is frequently used in the early years. It can be used to describe every eventuality, planned or unplanned, and has almost become a throwaway term that has lost its identity, although the debate surrounding the meaning of play is constant (Sutton Smith, 1997). Play should be individual to a child and be focused on what emerges from what they are doing when they play. In practice this means that practitioners need to observe and listen to children when they are engaged in play and provide both the physical and social space for children to make choices and use their initiative (Pramling Samuelsson and Fleer, 2008). An important aspect of supporting quality play is to recognise children's choices and reflect on why those choices have been made to inform future planning. Listening to children's views is vital to establishing a child-centred environment which can support quality play. However, Greene and Hill (2005: 18) identify that 'it is important not to just pay lip-service to the idea of listening to children or exploiting what is learnt from children about their lives in ways that meet the adult agenda only'. Consequently, practitioners need to be aware, not just about how they listen to children, but also be clear about the rationale for advocating children's autonomy and voice.

Foundations of quality play

Van Oers (2003) argues that quality is a contested concept that can never be absolutely defined. It is based on underlying values and beliefs of those making judgements and on perspectives that they prioritise; for example, a parent may view play very differently from a practitioner because practitioners have different experiences of what play constitutes and what children gain from their explorations. Howes et al. (1992) argue that quality can be equally seen through two contrasting lenses: structure or process. Examples of quality based on the perspective of structure include concrete and tangible aspects of quality which are easy to identify and control, such as child to adult ratios, group size or training and qualifications of practitioners. In contrast, examples of quality from a process perspective are more challenging to define because they rely on subjective interpretations, such as the values and beliefs of practitioners, knowledge and understanding of play or a sensitive disposition towards children's individual needs. In practice it might seem that structure and process can be mutually beneficial; for example, if an aspect of quality is the size of the group, then an argument could be made that the smaller the group the more individual attention a child could receive, consequently supporting the process of building positive relationships. However, the connections between structure and process are more complex.

Play is a construct where the pedagogic opportunities for children have been extensively documented (Wood, 2010; Fromberg and Bergen, 2006), but pinpointing the exact reasoning, or articulating the essence of play in concrete terms is more problematic (Hughes, 2001; Guilbaud, 2003). Quality can be seen in much the same way. We understand the concept of quality when we experience it, but when asked to describe a quality experience, explanations are very personal and subjective. Dahlberg et al. (1999) suggest that although it is more comfortable to seek concrete answers, there is always an element of uncertainty. Consequently, it can be argued that personal perspectives, reflection and being influential in children's development are the ingredients that make early years so vibrant and interesting. Dahlberg et al. differentiate between judging quality as a structure, where judgements are made through externally determined norms such as policy frameworks or guidelines, and process-oriented 'meaning-making' of what is happening to a child in play, how this links to other areas of development and what it might mean for future play opportunities. In an environment where play supports meaning-making, it is also essential that practitioners engage in reflection and interpretation: being involved in constructive debate and discussion to understand the context of play and what is happening within it. Sylva and Pugh (2005) argue that interpretative variations of children's play can cause tension between practitioners who observe play in different ways. They advocate for active and reflective discussion about play, but suggest that variations in values and beliefs about play can lead to inconsistencies in the way play is observed and interpreted. Consequently, the foundations for quality play focus on developing a process-based approach, and the question, how can *quality play* be cultivated?

Cultivating quality play

Figure 5.1 illustrates the 'roots' of quality play. These are derived from a child-centred ethos which Katz (1994) suggests is where children are supported in exploring their own interests to make connections with their environment and those within it. Katz (1998), like Dahlberg et al. (1999), also suggests that in observing play practitioners are influenced by structures that include a whole range of 'top-down' perspectives relating to curriculums, policies and procedures. This sometimes overshadows how practitioners want to organise their setting or the overall ethos they want to achieve. The pressure from top-down perspectives can detract from ensuring that play stays at the centre of practice. In contrast, children naturally generate a 'bottom-up' perspective because they are concerned with their own interests and explorations. The motivation for their explorations may not be immediately clear but in developing an understanding of the 'roots' of play, practitioners can place greater emphasis on a bottom-up perspective to ensure that child-centred, free play can occur.

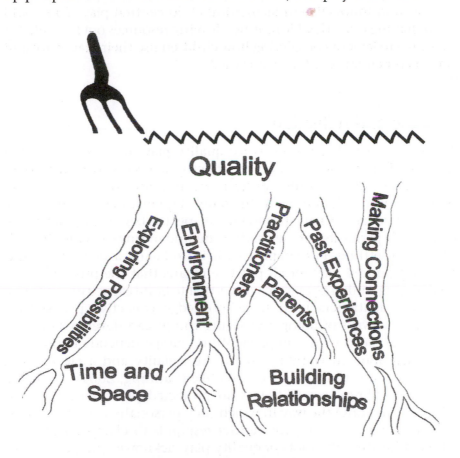

Figure 5.1 Cultivating the roots of quality play

The 'roots' in Figure 5.1 are essential in providing a solid foundation for quality play to grow and develop. They reflect a child-centred perspective where all the roots start with children's individual needs and unique qualities at the forefront of practice. By focusing on the roots, practitioners emerge as proactive in facilitating play opportunities because they develop meaningful interactions with children and parents based on evolving shared values and beliefs. The roots are also interconnected. Practitioners need to build relationships with parents and carers so that they can have an understanding of children's past life experiences. This information provides insight into the way in which children play and how they go about making connections with other children. The roots are interdependent and have implications for each other. For example, supporting children in exploring different possibilities through their play can only be cultivated if there is time and space to do so. In establishing the roots of quality play, settings and practitioners have to be prepared to be flexible and innovative in facilitating child-centred play. This could mean having more flexible routines, leaving resources out for children to return to later or considering how children use their play space and how its potential could be maximised.

Change and reflection

The role of planting the seeds for quality play to grow is therefore much to do with the ability of the reflective and sensitive practitioner who is aware of the fragility of seedlings and how roots can be easily damaged in their handling. As the roots of quality play begin to grow and attitudes and beliefs start to take shape, the beginnings of change can start to permeate through staff teams and settings. Change in itself can be unsettling, but coupled with introducing a dedicated focus on child-centred play for all practice means that the process is also challenging. Fullan (2005) recognises that to build capacity for positive change practitioners need to acknowledge collective perspectives so that new ways of doing and seeing things can develop alongside each other. Successfully implementing change depends upon open communication in working towards collegiality and a clear vision of what child-centred practice looks like (Canning, 2009). To ensure that the seedlings for quality play are protected, practitioners need to recognise not only the way in which they personally react to change, but how, as a collective, the setting responds to change. Therefore, when cultivating the roots of quality play, acknowledging a need for change may be a central aspect of developing quality practice. This does not just mean organisational, regulatory or curriculum change (though these aspects are significant). It also means changes in children's lives, for example transitions between settings or a change in family circumstances. This means that not all roots are strong and positive. Some children may have had difficult past experiences where their capacity for building relationships, among other things, has suffered. Consequently, a reflective practitioner who understands a child's background and culture is able to nurture play experiences, taking the lead from what the child is doing in their free play. This is not always an easy experience for the practitioner and is illustrated in the case study below. The names of the practitioner and child have been changed to protect anonymity.

Case study: Nassim

Nassim, aged four, has been attending a private day nursery for the past year. His key worker, Paul, knows that Nassim has recently found out that his 'big brother' was killed in Afghanistan while on active duty with the military. The family are devastated, but have only spoken in a limited way with Nassim about their feelings, explaining to the nursery that they don't want to upset him. Although Paul has tried to explain the importance of involving Nassim in their grieving process, the family are apprehensive and want more time to prepare themselves and Nassim.

The setting operates a child-centred policy where children are supported in making their own play decisions and engaging in free play. They pride themselves in having a holistic view of the child and take time to observe, liaise with parents and other professionals. Consequently, they are attuned to the fact that Nassim has started to play more aggressively with his peers, seemingly recreating a rough and tumble game over and over again where he arranges his friends in a line and then runs into them with his arms wide. Sometimes the others, foreseeing the crash, move out of the way, and it then becomes a chasing game with Nassim running around the perimeter of the outside space. In other variations, the children tumble to the ground and then Nassim curls up in a ball and stays still, then suddenly jumps up and starts the game over again. Paul, in detailed discussion with his colleagues and Nassim's parents, thinks that he is trying to make sense of his feelings of loss through his play.

Paul and his colleagues feel that Nassim is using play to work through some of the emotions he is experiencing after the loss of his brother. The practitioners interpret the rough and tumble play as a way in which Nassim can take control, stay at the centre of the action and add elements of risk. Haanpaa and Ehrs (2009) and Langsted (1994: 42) argue that a central aspect of play is that it is linked to emotions and supports children in understanding and coming to terms with real life situations. They recognise children as 'experts in their own lives' and argue that it is important not only to listen to what children say, but to notice what they do. Guss (2005: 233) suggests that when left to their own devices, children 'seek and construct form and meaning that have immediate significance for them'. Consequently, Nassim, through play, is constructing knowledge, ideas and meaning to come to terms with his feelings. Having a holistic view of the child and knowing what is going on at home and how that manifests itself in the setting is an essential component of supporting children in their play. Understanding children's individual needs and enabling children with the opportunity to explore their emotions and sense of who they are form essential components of child-centred play (Sutton Smith, 1997). It also means that practitioners can make informed judgements about the quality of play based on knowing the 'roots' of the situation.

Child-centred environments

The environment is another 'root' in cultivating quality play. In being proactive towards children's play the indoor and outdoor spaces need to be flexible, using natural materials and resources to enable children to use them in open-ended ways. If children are involved in developing their play space, they have a sense of ownership and can feel that their voice is being heard and valued. Nicholson (2005) advocates for children's involvement in designing play spaces to build capacity for creativity and inventiveness. A play-based environment which emerges from a child-centred ethos reflects processes such as trial and error, consultation and collaboration in order to make decisions about what works and what needs to be developed. Kadis (2007) advocates that an effective play space provides a variety of resources, giving children an element of choice and freedom to revisit and explore different ways to use materials. O'Brien (2009) agrees that supporting an interactive environment affords children the opportunity to try new things and have different experiences or build on existing ones.

In 2008 Play England and 11 Million commissioned a review, led by the Children's Commissioner for England, that led to a report, *Fun and Freedom: What Children Say about Play in a Sample of Play Strategy Consultations*. Children were asked about crucial elements of play provision. They responded that freedom, physical activity and areas that encourage socialisation, and opportunities to engage in active outdoor play were important to them. Children's views also support research undertaken by Brown (2009) who interviewed 6,000 people about their childhoods. His findings suggest that a lack of opportunity for unstructured, imaginative play can keep children from growing into happy, well-adjusted adults. He suggests that free play is critical in order for children to become socially adept, be able to cope with stress, and develop cognitive skills such as problem-solving (cited in Wenner, 2009). Vickerius and Sandberg (2006) argue that play has an intrinsic link with the environment because it informs what children can do. A flexible and dynamic environment with open-ended resources can support children to use their imagination and inventiveness in ways that practitioners might not have thought possible. Stimulation of new play possibilities emerges through a physical and social environment that reflects a proactive response to listening to children through their actions and reactions (Kyttä, 2006).

Langston and Abbott (2005) argue that children's play is influenced by their immediate environment as they use the resources available to them to develop and master skills, explore and problem-solve, be creative and use their imagination; this view is supported by Rosie Walker in Chapter 7. The environment is therefore an important 'root' for quality play, because outside of play children may not have a voice in how their experiences are structured or who they socialise, participate or communicate with (Skar and Krogh, 2009). Listening, observing and having a sensitive rapport with parents and children are also fundamental parts of quality provision. Engaging children in discussions about their environment, their play and understanding their view is essential to them feeling valued. In which case, practitioners need to have knowledge and understanding to make informed decisions about the ideas that work for a play-based environment and those that are impractical.

Introducing quality principles for play

In exploring the roots of play (Figure 5.1) and discussing how the seedlings of quality play can be nurtured, it is important to consider how these seedlings continue to grow into 'trees', with a strong 'trunk' of quality play provision. Having a child-centred ethos alone is not enough to ensure that quality play is established and central to practice. It requires practitioners to take on a multi-faceted role in seeing play as an evolving process, central to all aspects of early years practice. Consequently, it becomes possible to introduce the following quality principles for play, which are based on literature and research surrounding play. Underpinning these principles is a view that play requires not only individuals, but proactive teams of practitioners, settings and wider communities involving parents and carers, to ensure the growth of quality play. The eight principles are as follows:

1   There are many different perspectives of play and therefore it is essential to have knowledge and understanding to make informed decisions about how play is facilitated in settings.

Early years practice has seen a marked increase in the amount of training and continual professional development over the last ten years (Miller, 2008). Much of this training relates to 'top-down' perspectives in implementing curriculums, policies and new initiatives (Katz, 1998). However, this knowledge is essential in considering the principles on which decisions are made, how they are informed and the position they take on play. It is not enough to obtain knowledge; it is the way in which it is used that impacts upon children's experiences, learning and development.

2   Ensuring that settings are committed to a holistic view of the child, that this is communicated to parents and that considera-tion is given to how practitioners respond to developments from outside agencies.

Having a holistic view of the child is imperative. All children have different needs and qualities, so quality play opportunities should reflect and celebrate the diversity of children. Although settings work within boundaries and restrictions, there is flexibility to respond to individual children's needs and to consider their whole experience, not just within the setting but also how they are influenced by their family and community. Parents and carers provide the link between home and setting, so they are central to understanding children's individual circumstances. In responding to developments from outside agencies, the child's experience should be at the forefront of any decisions made about implementing new initiatives. Where one child may excel, another may struggle. This is a central consideration when supporting child-centred, free play, because the way in which individual children respond to play situations will be different. Observation and consideration of children's holistic needs will indicate areas where children may need further support. However, Veale (2001) argues that play creates the circumstances where holistic development can flourish.

3   Being proactive in prioritising and promoting a play-based curriculum that underpins all learning in an early years setting.

Each of the curriculum frameworks within the four nations of the UK propose that play should be a central aspect of practice (DCELLS, 2008; DENI, 2008; DCSF, 2008; Scottish Government, 2008). It is how play is interpreted in practice that sparks debate. The rhetoric of policy and reality of practice means that practitioners have to justify their position on play and then follow through in the actual practice that takes place in the setting. Consequently, discussions about play can become defensive in justifying quality provision. This quality principle demands scrutiny of values and beliefs, because it is one thing to say that the setting is proactive in prioritising play and another to see it in practice. This principle is loaded with 'what ifs' and will mean different things to different settings. It might be a 'work in progress' for many or an aspiration to strengthen underpinning attitudes in staff and parents, but it is an essential component in the process of quality play.

4   Creating opportunities to cultivate relationships with parents and carers so that practitioners have an understanding of children's ethnicity, background and culture.

Michael Reed and Alison Murphy in Chapter 10 discuss the importance of parents in considering quality improvement. This principle relates to how parents can help practitioners understand and sensitively interpret what children are doing when they play. Placing play at the centre of discussions with parents will reveal a wealth of information that enables play to be better understood and also contributes to the second principle, the importance of having a holistic view of children. The life experiences of children emerge through child-centred, free play and in gaining knowledge about children's ethnicity, background and culture; their actions and reactions in play can help practitioners find connections between children's experiences.

5   Facilitating an environment that supports children to access new experiences, take risks and challenge their own perceptions.

Quality play emerges when children are able to accept challenges and take risks within a contained environment. Mitchell et al. (2006) agree that risk in play is essential, but it should be managed through finding a risk level that is appropriate and acceptable to practitioners, parents and children. Gill (2007) and Lester and Russell (2008) are concerned that many western societies are becoming risk-averse, which is leading to an overwhelming culture of fear. However, in taking risks children have the opportunity to push their own boundaries and limits. They can develop a better understanding of their physical environment, but also what they can achieve when they take a risk, try something new or set themselves a challenge.

Little and Eager (2010) argue that practitioners should be proactive in risk management so that negative consequences associated with risk are minimised and so children have the opportunity to access new experiences.

6   Ensuring practitioners have a 'can do' disposition towards children that allows them to demonstrate success, experiment within their environment and communicate with others.

A favourable disposition towards child-centred, free play is essential to its success in any setting. Children require support from practitioners who can make anything possible in their play by using their imagination and creativity. This requires the practitioner to follow the child's lead, improvise and suggest meaningful ideas within the context of play that will sensitively support their learning and development. Kalliala (2009) refers to a 'can do' practitioner as an 'activator' who can identify children's interests and support subsequent play to develop. Adopting a 'can do' disposition also requires an awareness of the power relationships that exist between children and adults in play situations and also the power that exists between children when they play. It must be the child's experimentation with the support of the practitioner, rather than the practitioner leading the child in a play situation that they think the child wants to participate in.

7   Ensuring that practitioners are sensitive to children's invitations to join their play so that practitioners remain in children's games and follow their agenda.

When children engage in play it belongs to them (Sutton Smith, 1997). Children use play to create opportunities to develop their own fantasies, games and rules. They may invite adults into their play where practitioners have an important role to watch, listen and respond appropriately to the play that is evolving. It is imperative that practitioners have the confidence to stand back and wait for an invitation by the child, so that the play remains child-centred. There is an established continuum of practitioner involvement in children's play, from unstructured play without adult support to highly structured adult-directed activities (DCSF, 2009). But when children invite adults into play it is essential that children remain in control and that practitioners do not move towards the structured end of the continuum or enforce consciously or subconsciously any preconceived ideas about what should happen in play.

8   Creating opportunities for reflecting on practice, and building strategies to ensure that practice remains child-centred and play-based.

A key element of quality play is reflection on personal practice and on the play experiences of children in the setting. It is important to recognise and analyse current working practices and understand how they have evolved and on what basis they were implemented. It is also important to look to the future and consider how quality play can become established through growing quality principles for play. The voice of the child is a key element in ensuring that a holistic and child-centred approach to play is maintained; these voices need to be heard and listened to because they act like a compass to keep quality play on track.

These eight principles form the 'tree trunk', which has its roots in the bedrock of quality play (see Figure 5.2). They are interdependent upon each other and fit together; for example, it is difficult to be a sensitive practitioner without being reflective. As a collective they are a strong body on which to base quality play. They also allow for flexibility, because each principle is based on a process of development within a setting or individual practice. Consequently, there are different degrees of being proactive to prioritise a play-based curriculum based on circumstances, type of setting, opinions of colleagues about play and learning or the way in which the setting is organised and managed. Each principle has a context, yet the journey to embedding these play principles in practice and making the quality play 'tree' strong and secure is dependent on the values and beliefs and subsequent practice of the setting.

Recognising the child's agenda

The branches and leaves form the final part of the quality play tree (Figure 5.2). They are the processes that emerge from individual children's free play, which continue to evolve, as play evolves. Play is not a single event, but a continuum of opportunities. Play changes and 'grows' as children develop. In providing practice that focuses on growing a 'tree trunk' of quality play principles, the branches and leaves of the tree provide endless possibilities for children to experience and learn. For example, every time a child begins a new play experience they will draw on new influences or build on previous play. Children incorporate the world around them into their free play, which stimulates qualities such as curiosity, creativity and

Figure 5.2 The quality play tree

inventiveness. The process of play can also evoke strong emotional responses. It is essential that a sensitive and reflective practitioner applies the quality principles of play to remain child-centred, yet also knows when to implement strategies to evaluate children's experience and provide a supportive structure to facilitate the development of their play choices (Canning, 2011). Hughes (2001) argues that children do not have enough opportunities to follow their own agendas because of the pressures of everyday routines and activities. In free play Whalen (1995) reasons that children can explore a sense of who they are, especially when they develop relationships with their peers and explore social situations together through play. Quality is then defined by the value placed on recognising the child's agenda, how sensitively observations of play are interpreted and what the information is used for.

The 'interconnectedness' between children's play and learning, 'where in any play situation, a learning opportunity is also evident' (Canning, 2010: 34), arguably could extend to incorporate quality processes. Cultivating the 'roots' of quality, applying them into the quality principles of play and observing the qualities that emerge from child-centred play provide a foundation for connecting play, quality and learning. These connections rely on working within a process, the degree to which the connections are valued and the extent to which the quality principles of play are applied in a setting. The interconnectedness also relies on learning being seen as a process and not as an outcome. Consequently, when children are supported by quality 'roots', the principles of play that grow are strengthened and have the opportunity to cultivate child-centred *quality play*.

Summary

In exploring some of the issues related to quality and play, this chapter has suggested quality principles for play as a way to develop practice that will support the 'roots' of quality. The perspective of child-centred or free play has been considered, with emphasis placed on children engaging in their play environments to support their interests and explorations. The child's voice has been a strong focus, arguing for autonomy and individual choice as central to quality play. Concepts have been explored on the basis of process rather than achievement or outcome focused play. Children's choice and autonomy, the way in which they are consulted, and what happens in their play environment are central arguments to providing opportunities for quality play experiences for all children.

References

Canning, N. (2009) 'Empowering communities through inspirational leader-ship', in A. Robins and S. Callan S. (eds), *Managing Early Years Settings*. London: Sage.

Canning, N. (2010) 'Play in the early years foundation stage', in M. Reed and N. Canning (eds), *Reflective Practice in the Early Years*. London: Sage.

Canning, N. (2011) 'Celebrating children's play choices', in N. Canning (ed.), *Play and Practice in the Early Years Foundation Stage*. London: Sage.

Dahlberg, G., Moss, P. and Pence, A. (1999) *Beyond Quality in Early Childhood Education and Care: Postmodern Perspectives*. London: Routledge Falmer.

Department for Children, Education, Lifelong Learning and Skills (DCELLS) (2008) *Foundation Phase Framework for Children's Learning for 3 to 7-year-olds in Wales*. Cardiff: Welsh Assembly Government.

Department for Children, Schools and Families (DCSF) (2008) *Practice Guidance for the Early Years Foundation Stage*. Available at: http://publications.education.gov.uk/eOrderingDownload/eyfs_practiceguid_0026608.pdf (last accessed 2.12.10).

Department for Children, Schools and Families (DCSF) (2009) *Learning, Playing and Interacting: Good Practice in the Early Years Foundation Stage*. Nottingham: DCSF.

Department for Education Northern Ireland (DENI), Health, Social Services and Public Safety (2008) *Curricular Guidance for Pre-school Education*. Northern Ireland: Council for the Curriculum, Examinations and Assessment.

Fromberg, D. and Bergen, D. (2006) *Play from Birth to Twelve: Contexts, Perspectives and Meanings*. New York: Routledge.

Fullan, M. (2005) *Leadership and Sustainability*. London: Sage.

Gill, T. (2007) *No Fear: Growing Up in a Risk Averse Society*. London: Calouste Gulbenkian.

Greene, S. and Hill, M. (2005) 'Researching children's experience: methods and methodological issues', in S. Greene and D. Hogan (eds), *Researching Children's Experiences: Approaches and Methods*. London: Sage.

Guilbaud, S. (2003) 'The essence of play', in F. Brown (ed.), *Playwork: Theory and Practice*. Buckingham: Open University Press.

Guss, F. (2005) 'Reconceptualising play: aesthetic self definitions', *Contemporary Issues in Early Childhood*, 6 (3): 233–43.

Haanpaa, L. and Ehrs, C. (2009) 'Experts in their own lives: the voice and representation of children and young adults', conference paper, European Society or European Societies? European Sociological Association 9th Annual Conference, University of Lisbon, 2–5 September.

Howes, C., Phillipe, D. and Whitebook, M. (1992) 'Thresholds of quality: implications for the social development of children in centre based child care', *Child Development*, 63 (1): 449–60.

Hughes, B. (2001) *Evolutionary Playwork and Reflective Analytic Practice*. London: Routledge.

Kadis, A. (2007) 'The risk factor', *Play Today*, 60, November.

Kalliala, M. (2006) *Play Culture in a Changing World*. Buckingham: Open University Press.

Kalliala, M. (2009) '"Look at me!" Does the adult see the child in a Finnish day care centre?' conference paper, European Early Childhood Education Research Association 19th Conference, Strasbourg, August.

Katz, L. (1994) 'Perspectives on the quality of early childhood programs', *Phi Delta Kappan*, 76 (3): 200–5.

Katz, L. (1998) 'What can we learn from Reggio Emilia?', in C. Edwards, L. Gandini and G. Forman (eds), *The Hundred Languages of Children: The Reggio Emilia Approach to Early Childhood Education* (2nd edition). New Jersey: Norwood.

Kyttä, M. (2006) 'Environmental child-friendliness in the light of the Bullerby Model', in C. Spencer and M. Blades (eds), *Children and Their Environments: Learning, Using and Designing Spaces*. Cambridge: Cambridge University Press.

Langsted, O. (1994) 'Looking at quality from the child's perspective' in P. Moss and A. Pence (eds), *Valuing Quality in Early Childhood Services: New Approaches to Defining Quality*. London: Paul Chapman.

Langston, A. and Abbott, L. (2005) 'Quality matters', in L. Abbott and A. Langston (eds), *Birth to Three Matters*. Maidenhead: Open University Press.

Lester, S. and Russell, W. (2008) *Play for a Change: Play, Policy and Practice: A Review of Contemporary Perspectives*. London: Play England.

Little, H. and Eager, D. (2010) 'Risk, challenge and safety: implications for play quality and playground design', *European Early Childhood Education Research Journal*, 18 (4): 497–513.

Miller, L. (2008) 'Developing professionalism within a regulatory framework in England: challenges and possibilities', *European Early Childhood Education Research Journal*, 16 (2): 255–68.

Mitchell, R., Cavanagh, M. and Eager, D. (2006) 'Not all risk is bad, playgrounds as a learning environment for children', *International Journal of Injury Control and Safety Promotion*, 13 (2): 122–4.

Nicholson, E. (2005) 'The school building as third teacher', in M. Dudek (ed.), *Children's Spaces*. London: Architectural Press.

O'Brien, L. (2009) 'Learning outdoors: the Forest School approach', *Education 3–13*, 37 (1): 45–60.

Play England and 11 Million (2008) *Fun and Freedom: What children Say about Play in a Sample of Play Strategy Consultations*. London: National Children's Bureau and 11 Million.

Pramling Samuelsson, I. and Fleer, M. (2008) 'Commonalities and distinctions across countries', in I. Pramling Samuelsson and M. Fleer (eds), *Play and Learning in Early Childhood Settings: International Perspectives*. New York: Springer Verlag.

Scottish Government (2008) *Curriculum for Excellence: Building the Curriculum 3: A Framework for Learning and Teaching*. Edinburgh: Scottish Government. Available at: http://www.ltscotland.org.uk/Images/building_the_curriculum_3_jms3_tcm4-489454.pdf (last accessed 15 December 2010).

Skar, M. and Krogh, E. (2009) 'Changes in children's nature based experiences near home: from spontaneous play to adult controlled, planned and organised activities', *Children's Geographies*, 7 (3): 339–54.

Sutton Smith, B. (1997) *The Ambiguity of Play*. Cambridge, MA: Harvard University Press.

Sylva, K. and Pugh, G. (2005) 'Transforming the early years in education', *Oxford Review of Education*, 31 (1): 11–27.

Van Oers, B. (2003) 'Learning resources in the context of play: promoting effective learning in early childhood', *European Early Childhood Education Research Journal*, 11 (1): 7–26.

Veale, A. (2001) 'Revisiting the landscape of play', *Early Child Development and Care* 171 (1): 65–74.

Vickerius, M. and Sandberg, A. (2006) 'The significance of play and the environment around play', *Early Child Development and Care*, 176 (2): 207–17.

Wenner, M. (2009) 'The serious need for play', *Scientific American Mind*, February: 22–30.

Whalen, M. (1995) 'Working toward play: complexity in children's fantasy activities', *Language in Society*, 24 (3): 315–48.

Wood, E. (2010) 'Developing integrated pedagogical approaches to play and learning', in P. Broadhead, J. Howard and E. Wood (eds), *Play and Learning in the Early Years*. London: Sage.

6

Now we've got it, how do we know it's working? Evaluating the quality impact of technology in the early years

Linda Tyler

Chapter overview

This chapter focuses upon the fact that digital technology is here to stay in relation to the way it promotes children's development. It moves the debate forward about how children may or may not respond to technology, and argues that we should now move towards an examination of how such technology can enhance quality. It provides examples of good practice and stepping stones for digital technology in early years settings. It reflects on the way practitioners are using and developing technology to aid their own reflective enquiry and suggests that new technology forms part of professional development, communicating with parents, recording and developing practice as a means to enhance day-to-day learning.

Technology and children

A seminal moment in my life was the birth of my first grandchild, Olivia Grace. Her birth and subsequent development have encouraged me to revisit my own thoughts on how and why technology might offer quality experiences to children of all ages. It has also made me reflect on a recent interaction with my god-daughter. Three-year-old Molly loves chatting to everyone about anything, so for her birthday I bought her a toy mobile phone – a rather impressive one, as it looked real. She pressed buttons, put it to her ear, shook it and turned it over in her hands several times before expressing in rather loud tones: 'They forget the sim card, Auntie Lin. It won't work without one!' This immediately told me that Molly was already an 'expert' and frequent user of the real thing. Molly's mum later informed me that Molly used a mobile phone more often than a landline. More extraordinarily, when Molly was playing she would often pick up something to represent a phone: symbolic representation, as suggested by Piaget and supported by Feasey and Gallear (2001, in Hayes and Whitebread, 2006). Feasey and Gallear affirm that children's lives are surrounded by the products of the information and communication age; children not only live the technological age, they *are* the technological age. They argue that children today have access to real technology and suggest that this access provides a route into wider development and science. This is exampled by the way Molly reacted. Both Olivia and Molly have entered a digital world where technology has become part of their everyday life and daily routine. However, the example also raises questions about how we ensure that they have quality experiences with technology and that we take neither them nor their digital world for granted. This is not to suppose that children do not have positive experiences or to be critical of the time, energy and resources provided by many early years settings. It is to prompt reflection on the digital home/setting divide and how the inconsistencies in these experiences can impact on children's learning and development.

The Early Years Foundation Stage in England (EYFS) (DCSF, 2008) states that by the end of their early years education most children will achieve the early learning goal for ICT, which is that: 'Children should find out about, and identify the uses of technology in their everyday lives, and use ICT and programmable toys to support their learning.' After the experience with Molly I found myself thoroughly dissecting this statement and questioning how it might affect Olivia. I asked:

- In what ways can Olivia find out about technology?

- Can she identify or discriminate between its uses?

- What does Olivia 'use' in her and her family's everyday lives?

- How can ICT support her learning?

- Is this support offering a quality development opportunity?

- Does Olivia have access to these?

- Does she need access to these?

I also questioned her possible interactions with technology and the consistency of the digital experiences she will have. For example, from a digitally enhanced household, Olivia at the age of one will enter childcare. How will her digital biography marry with her experiences in the setting? Prensky (2010) informs us that she is a 'digital native' – a child who has been born and raised in digital environments; but will she migrate to the status of 'digital immigrant' – someone who is adapting to digital environments, not born into them – if she finds herself entering a perhaps more digitally passive early years environment?

The digital environment

Many decades after the introduction of ICT into early years settings, debates still abound regarding its impact on young children's learning (Cordes and Miller, 2000; Holloway and Valentine, 2003; Buckingham, 2004). All these views centre around the purpose of education, which has always been to prepare citizens of the future: to ensure that children can participate in society, develop a sense of community, enter the workforce and develop personally. However, 'fitting' technology and in particular digital developments into any framework is not easy. Technology is continually striding forward; therefore, we can predict that changes will happen swiftly, but we cannot begin to imagine how big these changes will be or what impact these changes might have on future generations. It is clear, however, that if the purpose of education is to prepare citizens of, or for, the future we cannot afford to be nostalgic and look back to a world that did not encompass such technologies. We cannot merely consider ICT as a learning benefit; we have to consider it as part of children's 'digital' nativity. We cannot predict what a digital future will look like but we can respond to it.

Before entering into a deeper discourse around technology it would be appropriate here to pause and think about why digital discourses are sometimes contradictory. Discourses on learning have existed for almost a century, with many strong theories being tested but remaining resilient. An example would be Donaldson's (1986) questioning of Piaget's work on developmental stages. Donaldson suggested that children of a younger age could carry out Piaget's tasks if presented with them within a 'familiar context'. However, Piaget's stages held and were later used as a basis for separating the national curriculum into key stages. The discourse surrounding technology is and always will be different. Technology is contemporary; it will always be of the moment, as new technologies continue to appear and move us forward even more quickly. For this reason, discourses around technology are as transient as technology itself – many are outdated after just a decade.

In their report, *Fool's Gold*, Cordes and Miller (2000) state that too often, what computers actually do is isolate children, emotionally and physically, from the direct experience of the natural world. In direct contradiction, Mansell (2008) found that overall, in terms of the relationships between communication, technology, and the organisation of relationships, new technologies appear to give rise to a mix of new forms of sociality and relationships that do not differ substantially from those found in offline settings. Research carried out by Marsh et al. (2005) into how 0–6 year olds spend their leisure time and the *Media Literacy* report for 8–11 year olds (OFCOM, 2006), offers further support to Mansell's view. They found that even very young children used technology in pairs or groups and that socialising around technology was one of the benefits of it. Both reports also found that contrary to popular belief, children were not sedentary when using technology but were in fact very active and had balanced 'diets' of technology and traditional activities through choice. Of course, it is clear that the work of Cordes and Miller is now out of date in digital terms, as technology itself has compensated for many of the issues they raise. For instance, repetitive strain injury has lost its claim to fame as a techno disability due to new ergonomic keyboards and wrist supports; and the recently introduced interactive Nintendo Wii encourages children to move and exercise rather than sit and stare at screens. Consequently, after one decade the discourse has changed because in this instance 'remedies' for technology ailments have been found.

It was clear that from birth Olivia liked and responded to sounds, and her parents wanted to support her development in this area. As 'Nanna' Tyler has an early childhood background and a penchant for ICT, Olivia was introduced to podcasts at eight weeks old; in particular to Storynory (http://www.storynory.com). By nine weeks Olivia showed clearly that she recognised changes in people's voices during the story and in particular loved 'Rapunzel, Rapunzel, let down your hair,' which always elicited a big grin (see Figure 6.1). Mum and Dad now download the podcast onto their MP3 player and Olivia has access to the stories whenever and wherever it seems appropriate to use them. Tyler (2010) identified the potential of podcasting in the early years, whether as a listener to or producer of podcasts. At ten weeks the television started to attract and sustain Olivia's attention, particularly the bright Disney figures and especially when they sang. Look at some examples in Figure 6.1.

In many ways this response from Olivia supports research by Roberts and Howard (2004) on children's engagement with television between the ages of 14 and 24 months. During the course of the study children exhibited very high levels of attention and concentration, as well as joining in with various activities. After just three more months Olivia was able to play with the TV remote and realised that pressing the buttons would have an effect. Initially this seemed to be as a result of playing with other toys with buttons that Olivia possessed, as she did not look towards the TV but stayed focused on the remote, waiting for it to react in the same way that her 'baby computer' played music and flashed lights when buttons were pressed. However, one day she noticed that the 'picture' had changed on the TV when she pressed the buttons and from this point she recognised that buttons on the TV remote made a difference to the picture on the TV (see Figure 6.2).

Piaget's theory of cognitive development is a valuable and helpful guide here. It helps, first, to assess the current level of thinking of Olivia, and second, to offer experiences that are suitable and appropriate to her level of thinking. In this example the experience offered was not directed but 'suggested' through making the TV remote available to Olivia simply to play with. This was done after observations revealed that she had learnt that pressing buttons caused a reaction in other contexts. Of course, Olivia will also have seen her parents use the remote but it is difficult to gauge whether or not she had learnt the purpose of the remote from watching alone. However, the activity builds a picture over time of her thought processes and eventual realisation of the link between the TV and the remote control. The EYFS (DCSF, 2008) advises that 'a child's stage of development should be gauged from observations of *consistent* and *independent* behaviour, *predominantly* from children's self-initiated activities' (my

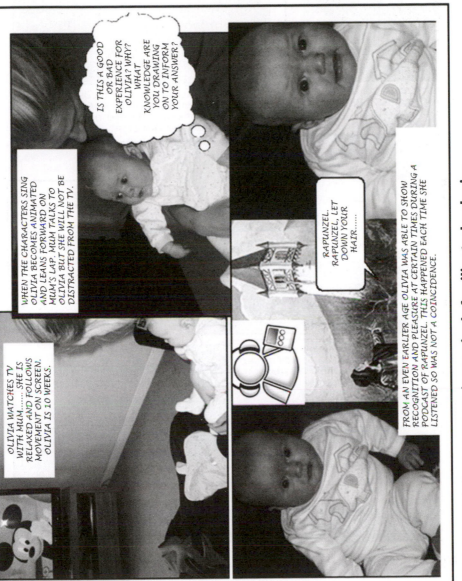

Figure 6.1 Olivia's exposure to increasingly familiar technologies

Figure 6.2 Olivia's journey to understanding a TV remote control

italics). I believe that Olivia's encounters with the TV remote offer this consistent and independent behaviour, but more than this they show her cognitively developing through the use of technology: that is, developing her thinking but in a different way – a way that will support her better in her digital future.

Olivia's early encounters with technology were not entirely her own as she was not personally pressing any buttons during the podcasting activity. Nevertheless, she was experiencing digital storytelling. Her parents' use of an MP3 player for music and stories will be something she continues to grow up with. It will become a familiar context (Donaldson, 1986). The podcasts do not stand apart from more traditional ways of accessing stories as Olivia already has stories made up for her, nursery rhymes and poems recited to her and stories read from books. But just as the latter are familiar to us, podcast stories will be familiar to Olivia and lots of other children born and raised in increasingly digital home environments. Indeed, Olivia's generation could be classed as emergent digizens (digital citizens), as not only does technology impact on their development, it also allows them to 'travel' wherever they want, physically or virtually, meaning that they can be citizens of both physical and virtual spaces – digizens, in fact.

Let me apply this notion of 'digizens' to another context in order to rationalise it. When we learn to read and write we become literate. Becoming literate does not mean that we need to read everything that is written; we cannot, it is both impossible and unnecessary as there are too many books in print and many of them will not interest us. How does this apply to becoming digitally literate? We need to consider the words 'digital' and 'technology' and how they are applied in today's world. It could be argued that there are as many 'technologies' as there are books, so what are we digitally literate with? Computers? Laptops? iPads? Mobile phones? The list is endless, but as with books, we cannot expect to be experts of, nor will we be interested in, all types of technology. We will become members of those communities of technology within a digital landscape that support and interest us.

Initially our literacy is guided by parent or practitioner choices, but as we develop we begin to migrate to literacy that interests or supports us in what we do. For instance, to 'chill out' I read romantic, historical novels. As an academic I continually seek to learn; however, I also need to switch off, and these novels enable me to do both, as I discover interesting historical facts within a story. You could say that I am a member of this 'genre' of story: that I have travelled to find my niche in a reading community. Thrillers do not interest me and therefore I will not visit the thriller community. However, I also need to read to inform my teaching role and at these times I travel to the academic readings that support the subjects I teach; I am then in a different 'literate' community. I am not static, as I move into and out of these communities as and when I need them. Traditionally, citizenship has been defined as 'belonging' to or being born into a place, however, with greater opportunities to travel we now have the choice to become citizens of a place other than our native home. In other words, citizenship can be transient; it can be moved and this is how digizens develop. They become members of those digital communities initially through parent then practitioner guidance and then through choice and/or need. These digital communities each offer a 'landscape of practice' and as digizens we may have several of these landscapes at a time.

Wenger et al. (2009) advise us to view learning not primarily as the acquisition of a curriculum but as the negotiation of an identity with respect to a landscape of practice, with a complex interplay of communities and boundaries. Though not a true interpretation of Wenger's work, let us reflect on Olivia's life so far using Wenger's notion of a landscape of practice but interpreting it by asking: what does Olivia's 'digital landscape' look like so far? I like to call Figures 6.3 and 6.4 Olivia's 'digiscapes' as they show her digital landscape pictorially and hence it is easier to compare her home digiscape with other digiscapes.

Figure 6.3 Olivia's digital landscape at 12 weeks old

Figure 6.4 How Olivia would currently meet technology at her local pre-school

Figure 6.3 illustrates the range of technology Olivia has already met at 12 weeks old. This image of Olivia's digital landscape is particularly important as it shows the technology pictorially so assumptions are not made about what the technology Olivia sees actually looks like. For example, the picture clearly reveals that other than her reading book Olivia does not own specific child versions of technology at this stage. Olivia's parents are both active users of technology, with Mum doing most of her shopping and banking online (hence Mum using the internet in Figure 6.3) and Dad using a range of technologies for work and pleasure. This digital landscape is very different from the landscapes Olivia's parents would have experienced at her age. Similarly my digital landscape at Olivia's age would only have contained a TV (without remote) and possibly a radio and landline telephone.

Buckingham (2007) argues that the use of technology in schools is actually quite out of step with young people's use of technology outside schools. Increasing numbers of young people find the use of technology in schools limited, boring and irrelevant – particularly when compared with the ways in which they can use technology in their leisure time. Buckingham recognises that bridging this gap –

this new 'digital divide' between home and school – will require a new, and less superficial, attention to young people's digital cultures. I would go further and suggest that this divide between home and the early years setting is often a 'black hole', with practitioner digizenship and child digizenship occupying landscapes that often cannot be recognised by each other. Let me give a very simple example. Most early years settings will have a digital camera. But how closely does the digital camera offered to children in a setting resemble the digital camera they have access to at home? Visits to settings have revealed that many buy a large, colourful and robust child version so that it cannot easily be broken, when in fact a simple neckstrap on an ordinary, more recognisable camera will do the same job. In other words, when we do try to bridge the divide or plug the black hole we do not always choose the right tools. In fact, let us look at the differences that already exist between Olivia's digital landscape and her local pre-school by combining the two digital landscapes. Figure 6.4 shows the technology presently used in the pre-school, with Olivia's familiar technology 'ringed' alongside it. Some technologies are missing. For instance, there is no computer of any type and the television has no aerial so will only play videos (not DVDs).

How can we ensure a quality experience and engage in quality improvement if our landscapes and hence our digizenship are so different? Plowman and Stephen (2003) believe that ICT used with young children is most effective if the distinctive nature of development in the early years is taken into account. The importance of play, the quality of relationships with other children and adults, and meaningful learning contexts are all central to the high-quality learning experiences we provide. A large, brightly coloured camera is not a familiar context for most young children.

Greenfield (2008: 48) notes the malleability of the brain in early childhood and shows concern regarding the ability of children's brains to make and lay down effective neuronal connections. Furthermore, she argues that the 'strongly visual, literal world of the screen' may stunt the development of the imagination and the child's developing construct of their own identity. However, Evangelou et al. (2009) suggest that there is empirical evidence of the benefits accruing to young children through interaction with ICT in their early years. This is supported by Smith's (2005 in Trushell and Maitland, 2005) longitudinal study of a young child and his use of CD-ROM storybooks. The study showed that there were positive impacts on his dramatic play, his proficiency in manipulating objects and his

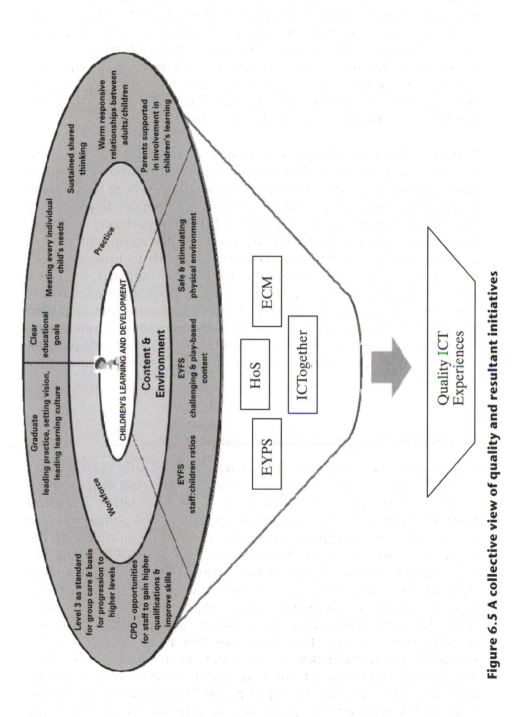

Figure 6.5 A collective view of quality and resultant initiatives

ability to symbolically represent elements from the storybooks. Evangelou et al. (2009) consider that making such conceptual links between different contexts requires 'holding ideas' which therefore offer the child a positive cognitive challenge. This is an advantage over and above the increasing command of the technological tools he was using. In other words, children are still developing physically and cognitively using ICT but it is different from how we learned. However, this difference is important to today's children as they will need to think differently to handle their digital futures.

Beastall (2008) noted that while children are ready for the digital era of education, teaching staff may need more strategic and pedagogical support in order to ensure that best value is obtained from technology. Clearly this support is crucial for adults if children are to encounter these stimulating experiences. Prensky (2010) is in harmony with this, using a digital native view of children and a digital immigrant notion of adults to illustrate his views. However, as with technology itself, the theory and ideas behind it will also become outdated. Prensky's theory of natives and immigrants has already been superseded by his digital wisdoms concept but he still offers no continuum of digital ability when clearly some adults are more techno 'savvy' than others. Nevertheless, adult understanding of the need for technology to be familiar and woven into play situations is crucial to achieving quality outcomes.

So can we recognise digital quality?

In 2007 the UK government carried out a review of early years settings to enable them to offer support for continuous quality improvement in line with the principles of the Early Years Foundation Stage and Every Child Matters (National Strategies, 2008). The review was also informed by the Quality Improvement Programme outlined by the Department for Children, Schools and Families (DCSF), Ofsted's Self Evaluation Form (SEF) and the National Quality Improvement Network's principles (NQIN, 2007). The concentric circles at the top of Figure 6.5 show diagrammatically what the New Labour government (1997–2010) thought were the key elements of high-quality provision in early years settings. But what does this mean in terms of QI strategies? The funnel below the key elements in Figure 6.5 are those programmes put in place to support success in terms of technology; although some were not developed particularly for use in early years settings but were aimed specifically at schools. For example, the

Hands on Support (HoS) initiative for staff training on using ICT with children was focused on school age rather than on pre-school age children, and the ICTogether programme, which delivered ICT training to parents and their children, was also targeted at schools.

So what is the way forward?

There is a need to define more clearly the words 'technology' and 'digital' when used in conjunction with early years experiences, as each word has a 'hugeness' that can cause confusion when planning for very young children. Conversely, though there are many manifestations of ICT in early years settings, the focus is mainly on computers. In other words the 'hugeness' of technology is trimmed down to a more manageable and recognisable ICT – that is, a computer. Early childhood settings value learning through play and child-initiated activities, whereas ICT tends to be viewed as a free play activity in which children decide for themselves when and how to use the computer.

When we do focus on a technology it also needs to be clear why. For instance, if we return to the statement in the EYFS (DCSF, 2008) – 'use ICT and programmable toys to support their learning' – three questions immediately pop into my head:

- What ICT?

- Which programmable toys?

- Why?

Of course, ICT use by young children needs to be supervised and vetted for suitability, as would be the case for any other book, toy or video. Observation, monitoring and recording of children's ICT activities is essential. Fischer and Gillespie (2003) recognise that for technology to have a positive effect on children's development, it must be used in a developmentally appropriate manner; though they also present strong evidence for the benefits of introducing young children to technology.

☐ Summary

Without being too self-serving and not intending any level of arrogance, I would suggest that just by reading this chapter you have started to reflect on how to improve quality for children: not necessarily because of my words, but because you are reflecting on practice by entering a debate about practice. ICT is becoming an ever-present element of the spaces occupied by young children. Technology is an important part of the lives of those people supporting young children's learning and development, whether as family members, carers, or early childhood practitioners. In Olivia's life so far this is undoubtedly the case. Donaldson (1986) espoused that children's early childhood education experiences should reflect and connect with their experiences in the wider world, that their experiences should take place within a familiar context. Therefore it must follow that ICT matters in early childhood because it already has an effect on the people and the environments that surround young children's learning and development.

References

Beastall, L. (2008) 'Enchanting a disenchanted child: revolutionising the means of education using information and communication technology and e-learning', *British Journal of Sociology of Education*, 27 (1): 97–110.

Buckingham, D. (2004) 'New media, new childhoods? Children's changing cultural environment in the age of digital technology', in M.J. Kehily (ed.), *An Introduction to Childhood Studies*. Buckingham: Open University Press.

Buckingham, D. (2007) *Beyond Technology: Children's Learning in the Age of Digital Culture*. Cambridge: Polity Press.

Cordes, C. and Miller, E. (eds), (2000) *Fool's Gold: A Critical Look at Computers in Childhood*. Available at: http://drupal6.allianceforchildhood.org/fools_gold (last accessed 2 December 2010).

Department for Children, Schools and Families (DCSF) (2008) *Practice Guidance for the Early Years Foundation Stage*. Available at: http://publications.education. gov.uk/eOrderingDownload/eyfs_practiceguid_0026608.pdf (last accessed 2 December 2010).

Donaldson, M. (1986) *Children's Minds*. London: Harper Collins.

Evangelou, M., Sylva, K., Kyriacou, M., Wild, M. and Glenny, G. (2009) *Early Years Learning and Development Literature Review*. London: DCSF and University of Oxford.

Fischer, M. and Gillespie, C.W. (2003) 'Computers and young children's development', *Young Children*, 58 (4): 85–91.

Greenfield, S. (2008) *The Human Brain: A Guided Tour*. London: Phoenix.

Hayes, M. and Whitebread, D. (2006) *ICT in the Early Years*. Buckingham: Open University Press.

Holloway, S. and Valentine, G. (2003) *Cyberkids: Children in the Information Age*. London: Routledge.

Mansell, R. (2008) *Communication and Information: Towards a Prospective Research Agenda*. France: UNESCO. Available at: http://eprints.lse.ac.uk/4265/ (last accessed 1 December 2010).

Marsh, J., Brooks, G., Hughes, J., Ritchie, L., Roberts, S. and Wright, K. (2005) *Digital Beginnings: Young Children's Use of Popular Culture, Media, and New Technologies*. Literacy Research Unit, University of Sheffield with BBC Worldwide and Esmee Fairbairn Foundation. Available at: http://www.esmeefairbairn.org.uk/docs/DigitalBeginningsReport.pdf (last accessed 2 December 2010).

National Quality Improvement Network (NQIN) (2007) *Quality Improvement Principles: A Framework for Local Authorities and National Organisations to Improve Quality Outcomes for Children and Young People*. London: National Children's Bureau.

National Strategies Early Years (2008) *Early Years Quality Improvement Support Programme*. Nottingham: DCSF.

OFCOM (2006) *Media Literacy Audit: Report on Media Literacy Amongst Children*. Available at: http://stakeholders.ofcom.org.uk/market-data-research/media-literacy/medlitpub/medlitpubrss/children/ (last accessed 2 December 2010).

Plowman, L. and Stephen, C. (2003) 'A "benign addition"? A review of research on ICT with pre-school children', *Journal of Computer Assisted Learning*, 19 (2): 149–64.

Prensky, M. (2010) *Teaching Digital Natives: Partnering for Real Learning*. California: Corwin.

Roberts, S. and Howard, S. (2004) 'Watching *Teletubbies*: television and its very young audience', in J. Marsh (ed.), *Popular Culture, Media and Digital Literacies in Early Childhood*. London: Routledge Falmer.

Trushell, J. and Maitland, A. (2005) 'Primary pupils' recall of interactive storybooks on CD-ROM: inconsiderate interactive features and forgetting', *British Journal of Educational Technology*, 36 (1): 57–66.

Tyler, L. (2010) '21st century digital technology and children's learning', in M. Reed and N. Canning (eds), *Reflective Practice in the Early Years*. London: Sage.

Wenger, E., White, N. and Smith, J. (2009) *Digital Habitats: Stewarding Technology for Communities*. Portland: C.P. Square.

7

Improving quality: do not forget creativity

Rosie Walker

> **Chapter overview**
>
> This chapter explores the world of children's creativity and argues that creativity is the 'lost' facet of learning for children in early years settings. Creativity can be lost the way it may so easily be subsumed within day-to-day activities that all practitioners have to do. It can perhaps be lost in terms of whether we are able to provide environmental opportunities for children to be creative, and also because to foster creativity we need to listen to children, listen to parents and ask ourselves if we can reflect and change in order to promote creative learning. This chapter argues that the link between creativity and quality must become more explicit to enhance sustainable futures for our children.

Exploring the importance of creativity

As the former leader of a large children's centre I can look back to the not too distant past when it was common practice for staff to put significant time into producing artwork for children to take home. The activity was pretty much directed by adults with the intention of showing parents just how creative children were. I wonder if we have actually moved far from this way of thinking, which relies largely on adult direction and intervention and is less concerned about the importance of practice being 'led by the child'. In more recent times the importance and value of the child's voice has started to take precedence. We now have, as an integrated part of quality provision, child-initiated play, practitioner strategies and planning that allows children to follow their interests, and in so doing develop richer learning experiences and enhance their creative potential. This is all well and good, but the question must be asked, how much of this is contributing to quality provision? How are these wonderful child-initiated aspirations dealt with by practitioners? How does children's creativity find time and space among the many practical day-to-day routine tasks that need to be done? (Percival, 2010). It can be argued that it is difficult to personalise a child's learning with a significant number of children to manage while dealing with other matters such as staffing issues, sickness and holidays. If we look at a typical setting, how much time do children really have to play? You may find it enlightening to observe a session within your setting and note exactly how much time children have to pursue their interests.

I suspect that this time is actually quite limited. Children are required to make a number of transitions – from inside to outside, to snack or lunch, to circle time, to key group time and story sessions (Sylva et al., 1980; Hutt et al., 1989). It follows that the deciding factor about the 'learning agenda' must be the way practitioners influence how the child's time is spent within sessions. When time is limited, 'quality matters', a point that is well exemplified by Kemple and Nissenberg (2000: 67) who state: 'Nurturing young children's creative potential is not a frill. It stands at the centre of preparing children for life.'

Evangelou et al. (2009) build on this view and suggest that a child in play demonstrates total concentration and absorption and that is how we know something special is happening within that child. It may be that the child is trying to make sense of a situation or solve a problem or make connections and it is at these moments that the child's creativity is most likely to be harnessed. Deep exploration through play can capture the magic of a child's world and this is echoed by Bechhi (1996, cited in Edwards et al., 1998: 91), who talks of 'mental excavation' where children's ability to connect ideas and create new meanings can occur.

Practitioner knowledge

If we agree that play is important, and in part the key that unlocks opportunities to enhance creativity, we need to understand what creativity means in practice. This involves looking at creativity as a concept more deeply, but this can be challenging, or as Rogers (2010: 130) describes, 'elusive'. There are many different definitions of creativity; for example, Torrence and Ball writing in 1974 state that it is the 'ability to perceive gaps in information and being able to think about these by creating hypotheses or actions that result in a solution' (cited in Karem et al., 2001: 248). This is a rather scientific definition, which may not apply itself readily to children's play, as children are unlikely to think in these terms. The National Advisory Council on Creative and Cultural Education (NACCCE, 1999: 30) tells us that creativity is an 'imagined activity fashioned so as to produce outcomes that are both original and valued'.

Others define creativity in terms of producing new outcomes (Rogers, 2010), which is attached to the notion of being of value (Seltzer and Bentley, 1999; NACCCE, 1999). Creativity can also be seen as a concept of quality where this is measured by a set of outcomes and targets. This can, however, reflect a rather mechanistic approach; it would be unfortunate to see creativity as a neatly packaged box of plans, targets, tasks, results and high expectations. Likewise, it should not be solely defined by prescriptive approaches such as those encompassing 'activities' that include music, dance, colour, texture or imaginative play. Activities are in danger of giving little credence to the process of learning and creativity, seemingly placing importance in defining the outcome. It would be more valuable to focus on the quality of the child's experience, which places value on assessing processes. This view is exemplified further in a rigorous and comprehensive review of the literature surrounding children's learning and development by Evangelou et al. (2009). A key finding of this review is that depth and not breadth of children's experiences is significant in empowering children's thinking, and deep understanding is more important than superficial coverage. The review highlights research into the analysis of children's problem-solving skills, with the results demonstrating that allowing children opportunities to explain how they solve a problem is more powerful than giving feedback about their performance and explaining why something was not correct. These findings also emerged in research on drawing and music-making, where children were more interested in the process than the final product. It seems, that responding to children's work effectively may be about understanding the processes they have been through rather than endorsing the end result.

Anna Craft has researched the concept of creativity in some detail and explains that 'possibility thinking' is at the heart of creativity. Possibility thinking is 'the means by which questions are posed or puzzles surfaced through multiple ways of generating the question "what if?"' (Craft, 2002: 1). She asks us to consider a creative environment that encompasses opportunities to engage in possibility thinking in which there is a change from a 'What is this?' question to a 'What can I do with this?' question (Craft et al., 2008). Her research highlights the importance of acknowledging 'question posing' and 'question responding', in both verbal and non-verbal behaviour, as having key roles in creative learning (Chappell et al., 2008). Giving children time, space, responsibility and freedom is essential in order for children to make their work visible. Duffy (1998: 18) views creativity as 'connecting the unconnected in ways that are meaningful to the individual concerned', explaining the importance of providing challenges and opportunities that allow creativity to develop.

Many different interpretations exist as to what creativity is and what it means in practice. For the child, in Malaguzzi's poem 'No way, the hundred is there', creativity is having a 'hundred worlds to discover, a hundred worlds to invent' (cited in Edwards et al., 1998: 3). It also means allowing children to have a voice in what goes on, to experiment, challenge and have opportunities to improve, because as Taguchi (2010) suggests, we cannot separate ourselves and learning from what is happening around us. However, there is a tendency within current education practice to 'present' the world to children. Taguchi advocates that children should explore through materials such as clay, and artefacts, so that they are not 'presented to the world' but are part of it as 'entangled becomings' (Taguchi, 2010: 47). Creativity is much more than providing activities; it is about providing opportunities (Craft et al., 2008). So can we arrive at a reasoned view about creativity and quality? Perhaps a clue comes from the National Children's Bureau Quality Improvement Principles:

> The approach based on the Quality Improvement Principles is not about com-pliance and ticking boxes against the DfES (DoE) agenda; rather it is about enabling local authorities and national organisations to deliver their vision for setting quality, adding colour, innovation and creativity to the national framework. (NQIN, 2007: 8)

It can be argued then, that the provision of opportunities for creativity to develop results from having a number of components in place:

- practitioner knowledge;

- a realisation that creativity is an essential part of learning;

- an environment that expands ideas rather than restricts what children can do;

- looking at how children learn (not measured competencies);

- recognising that creativity is only one part of developing quality experiences and by implication quality improvement for children.

This is not to argue that creativity is somehow special or more important than other aspects of learning; it should be an integrated part of what we all strive for – quality improvement.

Children just do it – adults like to find out why

Children play, laugh, move, communicate and enjoy exploring the world around them. Do they really need frames to be built around their learning? Creativity could be said to be the quality that an individual brings to activities. It might be best described as an attitude or an inner approach, for example how you look at something. It is perhaps often seen when children do not differentiate themselves from their surroundings. Children often start with the premise of wanting something, such as a ride on a train. They question at length and repeatedly start to make connections and add new ideas. The quality improvement cycle through the eyes of the child, represented in the inner circle of Figure 7.1, underpins the need to explore and use materials to pursue their quest. This model provides a useful framework for observing children and acknowledging their ability to build on past experience, consider new possibilities, or use what they have learnt to experiment, and then start the whole cycle again.

The inner circle suggests children can start or finish their play and learning anywhere within the four quadrants. The quadrants can revolve rather like a spinning top and the practitioner's actions represented in the boxes behind the circle can be applied to any of the four quadrants. This demonstrates the interrelationship between children and practitioners in enhancing and empowering children's

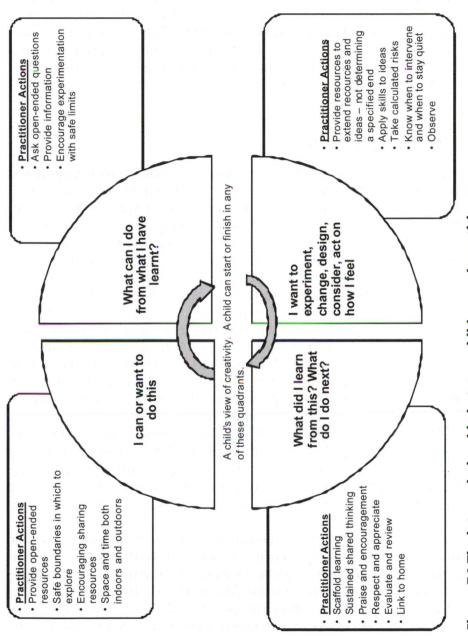

Practitioner Actions
- Ask open-ended questions
- Provide information
- Encourage experimentation with safe limits

Practitioner Actions
- Provide resources to extend resources and ideas – not determining a specified end
- Apply skills to ideas
- Take calculated risks
- Know when to intervene and when to stay quiet
- Observe

What can I do from what I have learnt?

I want to experiment, change, design, consider, act on how I feel

A child's view of creativity. A child can start or finish in any of these quadrants.

I can or want to do this

What did I learn from this? What do I do next?

Practitioner Actions
- Provide open-ended resources
- Safe boundaries in which to explore
- Encouraging sharing resources
- Space and time both indoors and outdoors

Practitioner Actions
- Scaffold learning
- Sustained shared thinking
- Praise and encouragement
- Respect and appreciate
- Evaluate and review
- Link to home

Figure 7.1 The inter-relationship between children and practitioners

learning through their play and gives an indication of how the practitioner can best enhance creativity. Of course, no two children are alike and all may have their special brand of creativity. Practitioners talking about creativity will tell you that children make voyages of discovery. Children make links between ideas, imagination, objects and resources and one can almost 'see' their ability to reflect critically on ideas, actions and outcomes developing. What we can be sure of is that children need time in which to explore and immerse themselves deeply in play (Cremin et al., 2006).

Practitioners matter

A practitioner's life is not an easy one, involving balancing adult and child roles to maximise learning and development. It is quite a skill to work alongside a child, to reflect on what they are doing without shaping or influencing them, and to participate in a child's reality rather than impose your own. Joining the world of the child requires a delicate balance. For example, it is important to accept and encourage the language a child is using without prompting for more vocabulary or more complex sentence structure, and allowing the child the freedom of silence in which to explore their world. It is often tempting to encourage using praise, without considering whether the praise is meaningful. Within the parameters of the setting, negotiations, ground rules and practical considerations are also important to maintain a healthy learning environment. Achieving the optimum combination of child-led and practitioner-led play is a delicate matter. In Figure 7.1 the outer squares build on the child's view of creativity within a quality improvement cycle and represent the practitioner's role during the child's cycle of creativity. Underpinning this is an awareness of the child's interests, having a trusting relationship with the child, showing interest and encouragement, and giving opportunities for children to express themselves in a variety of ways.

Consequently, attempts are continually being made to improve the quality of children's experiences and learning, both in what we might observe now and what might be developed for the future. This requires the ability to be reflective and take further the need to embrace changes in practice, attitudes, values and beliefs. Adaptability and a flexible approach are necessary to manage the demanding practicalities of the daily routine alongside enabling a freedom of exploration, as well as confidence within a role, supported by reflective practice, training and a shared ethos. But, I hear you say, does this mean just letting go and assuming that anything goes – allowing children free rein without boundary setting and accepting any sort of behaviour? This is not what I advocate. Learning has always had parameters and boundaries. Materials and the environment should be respected, as should the views of others. Encouraging children to accept the responsibility that goes with experimentation, challenge and enquiry is important and not a contradictory view of creative opportunities. But I recognise the counter-arguments:

- Expensive toys taken outside are in danger of becoming ruined.

- Cleaners complain that there is too much mess for them to clear up in the time they have allotted.

- Children are receiving 'mixed messages' about what they can and cannot do.

- Messages are sometimes not recognisable in terms of direct instructions or by easily identified adult disdain. They are instead subtle reactions to incidents, changes to the physical environment, looks, glances and even comments made to parents.

Do these sound familiar? If so, significant training, advice, observation and use of quality improvement are needed as the basis for change. Time and a collective culture shift are necessary in order to form a vision of what is required to foster creativity. By establishing a learning community that encompasses children, parents, staff, managers and governance, where everybody is confident that no one person has all the answers. Consequently, practice becomes a visible and rigorous examination of the setting to ensure that quality is developed. This includes the wider community, the whole staff, cleaners, caretakers and cooks, parents and children. Learning develops through listening and making positive relationships, sharing viewpoints and seeing different perspectives, which are powerful skills for participating in a democratic society and ensuring quality include making connections, changing ideas, and negotiating conflict.

The environment

Creativity cannot begin without discovery, and children need to explore and find out for themselves. The world is ever-changing and if we are to meet the needs of future generations new ways of thinking and new inventions must be uncovered. Children of the future will be presented with global problems that we do not know even exist yet and will be tested to their limits to find ways to survive. An increased life expectancy than previous generations means that independence, resilience, flexibility and adaptability will be essential skills. If a culture of exploration and experimentation is embedded at an early stage children may have more chance of creating a sustainable future.

The voyage of discovery requires children to be provided with the tools to facilitate creativity. One example is the idea of 'affordances' (Gibson, 1979). This approach suggests that children have an awareness of the possibilities afforded by environmental objects. Personal and environmental properties are used in reference to each other and what the environment offers to the child. This has been adapted by Nicholson (1971) as a theory of 'loose parts', which is a view of how landscapes and environments can be used to form connections. Children are given various materials which they use to move around, carry themselves, combine with other things, line up, redesign, take apart and put back together in any number of ways. Other materials and resources can be used alongside as desired; there are no specific directions so the child can decide on the direction the play takes.

Children need a wealth of time to develop their play. It can be difficult sometimes, particularly in pack-away settings such as church hall pre-schools, to give opportunities for extending play from one day to the next. Here it may be of help to do a sketch of the children's work for them to revisit. In settings where it is possible, try leaving work overnight and see if the children return to it in the morning, observing to see whether deeper levels of play emerge as a result. Grenier (2010) discusses the idea of core experiences where children are offered the same activities each day. For example, a cooking area could be set up with recipe books and ingredients where children can choose to cook. A similar gardening area might allow children to plant, grow and harvest all year round. Each time a child revisits a core experience opportunities are given for thinking and creativity to develop, encouraging further layers of complexity to be uncovered.

Such an approach can, of course, be challenging, as allowing children to create their own view of the world is sometimes problematic. It is useful to remember that when we are creating something new we are often at our most vulnerable, and open to fear of rejection or ridicule. Children too are likely to feel vulnerable and we as practitioners must be aware of the implications of this when tidying away work and clearing up, encouraging and joining with the child in affirming their work. How many times have we had to tidy up before children have finished, and not had the time to explore children's ideas, or omitted to acknowledge the vulnerability of the moment of creation?

Parents

Parents are an essential component of creativity, and indeed of their children's learning and well-being, as considered by Michael Reed and Alison Murphy in Chapter 10. Government guidance and research underpin the link between children's learning and development and the home environment (National Strategies, 2008). Therefore, it must follow that parents' views on creativity and how creativity is developed in the home environment are influential in nurturing children's attitudes and approaches to learning and exploration, and fundamental to improving quality (Evangelou et al., 2009). To understand how parents' attitudes to creativity can enhance the quality of settings, I undertook some research in a children's centre (Walker, 2010), interviewing parents about their own creativity and how they felt these impacted on family life. The centre was located on a primary school site in a ward designated by the Index of Multiple Deprivation as 'disadvantaged'. It runs a sessional nursery facility and a variety of family support and adult learning groups. All the parents felt that they had knowledge about their children's creativity that would be helpful for the setting to understand and incorporate into their practice. Family stresses and strains often made life difficult for some, but could lead to some very creative solutions. For example, as one parent said: 'Creativity can be inhibited by stress but sometimes needing to be resourceful can allow creativity to happen' (Parent A). Another stated: 'As a creative parent you should be willing to express yourself in what you do to show your child they can do what they want' (Parent B).

Families enhance attitudes for creative development for their children in several ways. Some seek children's opinions and involve them in making family decisions, which is likely to build confidence in problem-solving and independent thinking. In family situations children may also be encouraged to take risks and explore their ideas with different resources at their disposal. Parents who provide an environment rich in natural affordances, as opposed to a wealth of expensive toys, are as likely as any others to foster creativity within their children. One parent explained: 'It's making something from nothing, making a lot from a little' (Parent C). Surprisingly, it is not always the most loving families who empower their children to be creative. Kemple and Nissenberg (2000) discuss the parental traits that best encourage and influence creativity. They conclude that a rejecting parent may encourage their children to have a more rebellious attitude which can lead to challenging accepted norms and questioning accepted truths. While not advocating that parents should reject their children, it is perhaps those parents who are enmeshed in their children's lives or who overload their children with scheduled activities who may in fact be stifling creativity.

From the research it may be possible to gain a picture of the characteristics of parents able to foster a creative attitude within their children. Parents of creative children are likely to be concerned with their children's behaviour and interests but do not impose rigid rules or expectations. They may be able to tolerate their children making mistakes, while acknowledging that they will learn from these. Isenberg and Jalongo (1996) outline the characteristics of a creative environment and list seeking new approaches to problems and regarding differences of opinion as learning opportunities. This is supported by a parent who as part of my research said, 'It's important to allow time for children to think and comment on what they are doing, to give encouragement for them to think and do for themselves and be non-judgemental on their efforts' (Parent D). In light of this, the involvement of parents in developing creativity must be collaborative. Owen (2010: 191) argues creativity cannot be interpreted only as being attributed to individuals; we must consider the 'gravitational pull of relationships' and the 'need for the co-intentional imaginations of adults and children to embrace together attitudes of improvisation, keeping an eye open for the off chance, taking the occasional "non-assessed" risk and accepting the generation of and pleasure in "mess"'.

Parents can offer settings a wealth of expertise in the development of creativity. By becoming an integral part of the learning community and sharing ways in which they manage situations and life experiences they can enrich children's and practitioners' experience and opportunities. Parents need to be involved at the setting on every level. Within my research, parents often told me that they were not creative, yet they came up with a wealth of ideas about what makes a creative parent and how they encourage creativity in their children at home. Many pointed out that their success as creative parents came from the fact that they know what their children like, and surely this is essential information for settings. Parents pointed out the need to make a fun, happy and positive environment, with materials to enhance creative thinking, lots of support and encouragement and time to explore. Parents can be fundamental in aiding settings to

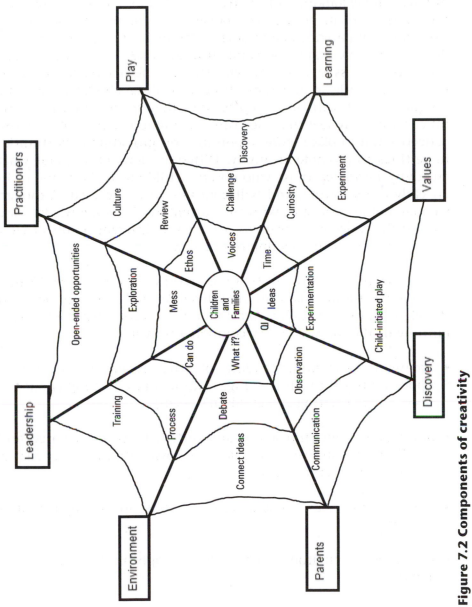

Figure 7.2 Components of creativity

create this environment and to help other parents to see that mess and risk-taking are important aspects of child development.

Earlier in this chapter I indicated the problem of trying to reconcile different understandings of creativity. It would seem that in practice the same problem occurs. The perspectives of practitioners differ from those of parents. Practitioners' very real concerns may include dealing with the many and competing demands of ensuring safety, minimising mess and dealing with the routine practicalities within timescales, while at the same time providing children with the unique support, care and opportunities they need. Parents, on the other hand, may feel that they can contribute much to offset these concerns and to place more importance on providing opportunities in settings to promote creativity. Different views exist about what creativity means by those who observe children in the home or in an early years setting, and will continue to be debated. Although we may not always agree with the current available knowledge base around the concept of creativity, discussing different points of view and perspectives can only improve quality.

The key components of creativity are represented in Figure 7.2 in a web, demonstrating that they are interconnected, and together with the eight strands of leading practice form a strong basis for under-pinning quality provision. Key components include:

- having a clear understanding of what is meant by creative opportunities through training, reading and reflecting about the needs of your setting and children's needs;

- developing leadership and teamwork that accepts change and is willing to consider new ideas and possibilities beyond what is expected by external agencies;

- seeing creativity as a process and a response to the opportunities presented;

- providing an environment that offers opportunities rather than activities;

- reviewing what goes on in a setting and engaging in a quality improvement cycle to consider change and improvement;

- recognising that parents are part of the process and that we should strive for a shared understanding about learning creatively.

Creativity is therefore rather like a web; it has many interconnected parts, and when these meet together they make a strong support for learning. This, of course, includes the practitioner, at the centre of the web. A harnessing of the voices of parents, children and practitioners adds rich dimensions to nurturing and can allow children's creativity to be fully recognised within quality frameworks. Reflecting on the need to make the link between creativity and quality explicit and valued is essential to our professional sustainability and survival, both now and in generations to come. To finish, here is one of my favourite definitions from an 'old' parent speaking to a 'new' parent at a children's centre; maybe they have got it right: 'Creativity is about being able to let a child loose. Not worrying about the mess it could make and the end product. Think about how much your children benefit and get out of it' (Parent E).

Summary

Throughout this chapter we have seen that creativity is an essential component of developing quality experiences for children. It is therefore vital that creativity is given our full attention and integrated throughout practice in order to achieve quality improvement within early years provision and to equip children with the innovation, skills and knowledge they will need to meet the challenges of the future.

References

Chappell, K., Craft, A., Burnard, P. and Cremin, T. (2008) 'Question-posing and question-responding: the heart of "possibility thinking" in the early years', *Early Years*, 28 (3): 267–86.

Craft, A. (2002) *Creativity and Possibility Thinking in the Early Years*. London: Continuum.

Craft, A., Cremin, T., Burnard, P. and Chappell, K. (2008) 'Possibility thinking', in A. Craft, T. Cremin and P. Burnard (eds), *Creative Learning 3–11 and How We Document It*. Stoke-on-Trent: Trentham Books.

Cremin, T., Burnard, P. and Craft, A. (2006) 'Pedagogy and possibility thinking in the early years', *International Journal of Thinking Skills and Creativity*, 1 (2): 108–19.

Duffy, B. (1998) *Supporting Creativity and Imagination in the Early Years*. Buckingham: Open University Press.

Edwards, C., Gandani, L. and Forman, G. (1998) *The Hundred Languages of Children: Reggio Emilia Approach – Advanced Reflection* (2nd edition). London: Ablex Publishing.

Evangelou, M., Sylva, K., Kyriacou, M., Wild, M. and Glenny, G. (2009) *Early Years Learning and Development Literature Review*. London: DCSF and University of Oxford.

Gibson, J. (1979) *The Ecological Approach to Visual Perception*. New Jersey: Laurence Erlbaum.

Grenier, J. (2010) 'EYFS best practice: all about planning around core experiences', *Nursery World*, 4 February.

Hutt, S.J., Tyler, S., Hutt, C. and Christopherson, H. (1989) *Play, Exploration and Learning: A Natural History of the Preschool*. London: Routledge.

Isenberg, J.P. and Jalongo, M.R. (1996) *Creative Expression and Play in the Early Childhood Curriculum* (2nd edition). New Jersey: Prentice Hall.

Karem, E., Kamaraj, I. and Yelland, N. (2001) 'An analysis of Turkish pre-school teachers' ideas about the concept of creativity and the activities that can foster creativity in young children', *Contemporary Issues in Early Childhood*, 2 (2): 248–56.

Kemple, K. and Nissenberg, S. (2000) 'Nurturing creativity in early childhood education: families are a part of it'. *Early Childhood Education Journal*, 28 (1): 67–71.

National Advisory Committee on Creative and Cultural Education (NACCCE) (1999) *All our Futures: Creativity, Culture and Education*. Available at: http://www.cypni.org.uk/downloads/allourfutures.pdf (last accessed 12 April 2010).

National Quality Improvement Network (NQIN) (2007) *Quality Improvement Principles: A Framework for Local Authorities and National Organisations to Improve Quality Outcomes for Children and Young People*. London: National Children's Bureau.

National Strategies Early Years (2008) *Early Years Quality Improvement Support Programme*. Nottingham: DCSF.

Nicholson, S. (1971) 'How not to cheat children: the theory of loose parts', *Landscape Architecture*, 62 (1): 30–5.

Owen, N. (2010) 'Creative development', in I. Palaiologou (ed.), *Communication, Language and Literacy in the Early Years Foundation Stage*. London: Sage.

Percival, J. (2010) 'Personalised learning: looking at children holistically', in J. Glazzard, D. Chadwick, A. Webster and J. Percival (eds), *Assessment for Learning in the Early Years Foundation Stage*. London: Sage.

Rogers, S. (2010) 'Supporting creativity', in J. Willan, R. Parker-Rees and J. Savage (eds), *Early Childhood Studies* (2nd edition). Exeter: Learning Matters.

Seltzer, K. and Bentley, T. (1999) *The Creative Age: Knowledge and Skills for the New Economy*. London: Demos.

Sylva, K., Roy, C. and Painter, M. (1980) *Childwatching at Playgroup and Nursery*. London: Grant McIntyre.

Taguchi, H.L. (2010) *Going Beyond the Theory/Practice Divide in Early Childhood Education: Introducing an Intra-active Pedagogy*. London: Routledge.

Walker, R. (2010) 'Children Centre Work Based Research', MA thesis, University of Worcester.

Section 3

Quality Improvement – Professional Practice

Quality matters because quality protects

Claire Majella Richards

Chapter overview

This chapter considers the concept of quality improvement in the context of children and safeguarding. An initial overview considers the emergence of such themes as 'quality assurance' and 'quality improvement' in the field of child protection and safeguarding within the early years sector. The impact of neglect on the quality of life and outcomes for children, where this is a key safeguarding concern within many vulnerable families, is explored alongside the need to consider the appropriateness and necessity of the provision of effective supervision for staff within early years settings. Supervision is integral to many professional disciplines and roles, who work with families with complex needs. It is regarded as an important aspect of quality assurance in promoting positive outcomes for children. Therefore, it could be argued that there is a case for the introduction of a supervision model for early years staff, in managing and reviewing the intricate aspects of their role in supporting children and families.

Note: There is a deliberate interchange between the phrases 'Early Years Professional' (EYP) in England, and 'early years practitioner'. The former denotes those individuals who have successfully completed a validation pathway to acquire Early Years Professional Status (EYPS), and the latter refers to all practitioners of diverse ranges of training and experience within early childhood settings.

The term 'quality' merits some focus to establish a fundamental understanding as to what this concept actually conjures for the early years practitioner. The context and ethos of their professional setting are important, particularly where they are working alongside other professional disciplines, as in the case of a family centre. Munro (2008) remarks that just as a social worker in the 1960s may have considered only whether a child's needs were being met, current practice insists that the concept of risk is integral to that assessment; arguably too, 'quality assurance' is part of that continuum. Therefore the knowledgeable, effective and competent early years practitioner plays a pivotal role within the inter-agency professional sphere, providing timely interventions to safeguard and protect a child while offering enabling support to parents and carers. The practitioner understands, through their commitment to proactive collaborative working and 'quality improvement' measures, that safeguarding is a quality issue that remains at the heart of good practice. However, there is a concern that the concept or terminology of 'quality' may become a matter of vague and meaningless semantics; at risk of a 'turn off' effect to its mere mention at staff meetings or training events, policy reviews or preparations for an Ofsted inspection. The challenge for any effective and astute early years manager is how to convince and lead staff to adapt a positive 'can do and will do' approach on an individual and team level. This is to ensure that the importance of quality matters at the forefront of all practice are consistent priorities of service safeguarding provision for children and their families.

Quality – an objectionable experience?

In considering the theme of 'quality' perhaps it is useful to allude to the experience of quality in the context of a consumer. On occasions, I shop at a very well known high street store, which has an outstanding reputation of consumer confidence for excellent customer care and high-quality products. As a free agent in the comfort and familiarity of this consumer environment, I have faith in knowing that the product I purchase, whether it is a Belgian chocolate pudding, a well-fitting bra, or a superb handbag, is fit for purpose. I have the best there is, while the interchange with staff is friendly and always helpful. In short, I will want to visit the store again soon. The outcome of this service is reassuringly positive (sometimes uplifting), and if asked whether I was content with the quality of service I received, my response would be a resounding 'yes'. Further, I know my rights as a consumer; if I am unhappy about my service, how staff have behaved towards me or if the product is faulty, I know that I can complain. I can express my concerns, having assurance that there will be measures in place to address the concern promptly and satisfactorily.

If this scenario is transferred to an early years setting, it would be interesting to imagine what the experience of the customer might be: that is, the service user – the child or the parent. The above scenario describes a free agent, who voluntarily accesses the services provided, with a confidence in expectations and outcomes. However, the meaning and importance of the issue of quality can depend on the perspective of the individual: the child or the parent. The reality for professionals, such as the early years practitioner working with a diverse range of children and families, means that some have complex needs and some are vulnerable. There are families who may be hard to reach, difficult to engage with or even hostile to professionals who are trying to help. In the case of a child who is subject to a Child Protection Plan there may be a clear expectation that the child attends a family centre for assessment, and that the parents participate in a parenting programme. By virtue of the provision of compulsory attendance, the service user is no longer a voluntary participant, but is there at the behest of the intervention and professional judgements of other individuals. The ensuing tensions between any feasible partnerships with parents in these circumstances can mean that efforts to engage with the child and family are difficult. Perhaps even the best-quality measures and provision will be of little consolation or assurance to angry or hostile parents. Even more so, the concern of how a child may perceive such inter-familial and professional dynamics is worthy of reflection. This is particularly poignant where a child is vulnerable, living with chaos and where neglect is a feature of their child protection profile. The scenario is a difficult position for the Early Years Professional (EYP), when there is much emphasis within the culture of early years on the promotion of positive partnership with parents. Similarly the EYP is required to be vigilant of the risk of overlooking the protective needs of the child in the event of staff collusion with abusive parents or concerted efforts to engage with evasive parents (Haringey LSCB, 2009). A child's needs may also be lost or subsumed within the assessment of a parent's own significant support needs (Cleaver et al., 1999).

In the case of working with children and families within an early years setting, it would be prudent for both manager and staff to consider how quality matters are visible to all who enter the setting. It may be suggested that quality is more than a paper policy; it must be organic to the culture of the setting, a tangible experience, a positive force affecting a way of being and behaving by the staff, a possession of attitude and promotion of professional values. Pilcher (2009) describes certain components of quality assurance within an early years setting as aspects of positive staff relationships, effective communication between colleagues and recognising and drawing from the strengths of colleagues. She refers to the issue of quality improvement within a setting as the ethos of team motivation and working collaboratively towards shared goals; in essence, 'quality improvements should be obvious to everyone – children, parents and staff' (2009: 93).

Quality matters for children of neglect

In a previous publication focusing on reflective practice, I highlighted some of the risk factors that can have a negative impact on parenting capacity on a long-term basis, producing some of the worst outcomes for children (Richards, 2010). This chapter has a deliberate focus on the experience of neglect as a feature of child abuse due to the long-term consequences on children, such as developmental delays or relationship difficulties (DCSF, 2009). Neglect is a common feature of abuse, blighting the lives of many children in the UK today (Gupta, 2010). It is because of the sometimes insidious nature of neglect and its pathological effects on early childhood experiences that this issue merits critical attention in the context of the EYP's role, in assessing need and promoting early interventions for a child and their family. It is important at this point to make a careful distinction between the difficult life experiences of parents within the realms of 'normality' – such as bereavement, illness or unemployment, which may have a temporary destabilising effect on the family – and the more chronic life-limiting and risk-causing factors that significantly impact upon a parent's ability to care for and respond appropriately to the needs of their child.

The number of professionals who have access to the privacy and intimacy of the family home is quite small; the general practitioner (GP), community midwife, health visitor or family support worker are examples of this particular group. This select and privileged group in the context of access are in a position to gain snapshot insights as to what life may be like for the children of a family. There may be signs of obvious neglect or failure of appropriate parenting, such as dirty and unkempt children, a filthy kitchen smelling of decaying food and strewn with rubbish, matted and soggy carpets, sparse or even the absence of basic furniture with no obvious signs of children's toys, or any visible toys may be broken or rendered useless. By stark contrast, a home may be pristine and clinically clean but with few signs of being child-friendly or permitting any degree of child freedom or play. Arguably, as these are descriptions of people's homes it could be viewed as improper or even unethical to impose personal or subjective opinions as to what is a 'good enough' home environment for a child, recognising that some parents do understandably struggle for a host of reasons. This argument carries some weight, but only to a point, as any case of the neglect of a child gives rise to an array of concerns that inhibit a child's emotional, psychological and physical development the effects of which, as mentioned above, can be long-lasting. The critical issue for any professional, including an EYP, is to avoid the perspective of 'rose-tinted spectacles', of being over-optimistic of parents' abilities to change and to improve the standard of care and home life for the child, despite long-standing evidence or knowledge of the family to the contrary.

Quality assurance – how it measures up in early years

There is scope for the early years practitioner in the role of a family support worker to take stock of what it would be like to be a child living in a particular family environment; gaining a powerful insight to know how it would feel to be in that child's shoes (Richards, 2010). The professional gut response, or intuition, is powerful if not unsettling, and it is this visceral response, alongside effective child protection guidelines and practice, that promotes and ensures effective and intelligent inter-agency responses. Munro (2008: 18, 26) refers to the strengths of 'intuitive reasoning' in terms of 'speed' enabling the practitioner to make judgements from a vast range of information and to act promptly in accordance with professional knowledge and wisdom. In addition to intuitive reasoning, Munro further alludes to 'analytic reasoning', which enables the practitioner to apply a 'more rigorous and explicit' approach to assessment in child protection and safeguarding. It is therefore essential that every early years practitioner, who may or may not be in the front line of everyday child protection work, recognises the crucial combination of these components as part of their critical reasoning and reflective thinking skills in dealing with child protection concerns.

One of the most important aspects of working with children and families where neglect is an identified concern, or causes concern as a risk factor, is the provision of timely, quality, child-focused assessments. This is in addition to assessments that measure parental needs and capacity, with a particular focus on the parent's insight to the life circumstances of the child, a willingness to engage with supportive services and, more critically, a motivation to change those aspects of ineffective parenting to 'good enough' parenting. There is little doubt that the complexity and implications of effective assessments for children and families is daunting, and is likely to test the professional mettle of any stoic individual working with families. The resistance factor of adults as parents is especially challenging to professionals involved in safeguarding and protecting children. However, Gardner and Cleaver (2009) are mindful that such adverse reactions by parents may be due to previous experiences with Children's Social Care, which may have been difficult, and feelings of defensiveness, anger or powerlessness may be triggered by a fear that they will lose their children. It is also possible that parents who vehemently push away outside agencies with abuse and threats of violence do so in order to avoid detection of child abuse and neglect. Despite these personal and professional anxieties the government report *Working Together to Safeguard Children* (DCSF, 2010: 133) makes sobering mention of the need for all practitioners to be guided by the principle enshrined within quality and effective working together practices: 'The child should be seen . . . his or her welfare should be kept sharply in focus in all work with the child and family.'

Parenting and parenting capacity

This chapter so far has made mention of 'parenting' and 'parenting capacity', so it would be useful to consider what is meant by these terms within professional understandings and dialogues. Jones (2001: 256) refers to parenting as 'the activities and behaviours of parents which are necessary to achieve the objective of enabling children to become autonomous. These activities and behaviours change as the child develops. Thus parenting as an activity is firmly yoked to child outcomes.'

It is recognised that the same principles of nurturing and enabling children are aspects of parenting that apply to all cultures and communities. There is a more convincing case, through evidence and research, that the involvement with parents in the decision-making process and evaluation of their child's needs will also be effective in continuing their engagement towards improving outcomes for children. In Quinton's words (2004: 172), 'Engagement is the first requirement of an effective service for parents and parenting. In this respect family centres have won the argument for their style of delivering many services to families.'

The matter of 'parenting capacity' may be more contentious as it can assume ineptness, but the balance of assessment, particularly through the Common Assessment Framework (CAF) (DfES, 2006), rightly places emphasis on the need for practitioners to look for the positive and protective factors of the child's home life and environment, in addition to presenting risk factors and concerns. The All Wales Child Protection Procedures (AWCPP, 2008: 65), for example, state:

> In order to make sensitive and well informed professional judgements about a child's needs, and a parent's capacity to respond to their child's needs, it is important that professionals are sensitive to different family patterns and lifestyles and to child rearing patterns that vary across different racial, ethnic and cultural groups.'

There is an additional note of caution for any practitioner that issues of respect for cultural diversity should in no way compromise the rights of the child: his or her safety and well-being. The EYP should work collaboratively with colleagues and other professional disciplines through implementation of a thorough assessment, which considers the strengths and limitations of the child's family. This approach, as a quality assurance measure, can go towards ensuring that the child's needs are identified in addition to the parents' abilities or motivation to respond to those needs. One important aspect of this quality assurance measure is the recognition of the exceptional commitment of early years practitioners to listening meaningfully to children. The voice of the child features prominently in their professional practice, and so this ethos or custom usefully informs the child's unique perspective as to what their needs are: how they see and experience life at home or, more importantly, what would help to make things better.

Leadership and management of team practice in child protection and safeguarding

The government's commitment and drive to continue to promote and improve the systems and services in place to protect and safeguard children will undoubtedly cause elements of both reassurance and uncertainty. Particularly in the shadow of austerity measures and public spending cuts, which will have an impact on critical services such a Children's Social Care, and on the children of families who are already perhaps the poorest and most deprived of our local communities. However, alongside these winds of change there remains a focus on what has been considered to work well, such as the

Common Assessment Framework (DfES, 2006) and the *Think Family* agenda (DCSF, 2009). The *Think Family* agenda promotes concerted practice to ensure that support provided by children, adult and family services are delivered and coordinated in a focused approach, to address problems that affect the entire family. The Munro (2010) review gives significant messages that will impact on the current professional practice of social work, and will have salutary messages for other professions, including the EYP.

The implications for the importance of joined-up thinking and effective inter-agency collaboration for early years teams are critical. However, in order to be effective in proactive and purposeful outreach to other services beyond the immediate setting, there is a need for the early years manager first to get their 'house in order'. It is recognised that management and leadership within an early years setting is challenging, and the duality of these roles for an individual requires a good sense of self-awareness and emotional intelligence (Goleman, 1998) in order to facilitate and delegate in accordance to need and demand. The effectiveness of early years managers is also vital in the context of quality improvements for service delivery to children and families.

The experience of being a team member and working within a team raises numerous and diverse experiences of colleagues' knowledge, values, emotions and expertise when facing issues that raise concern about the safety and welfare of a child. In the context of the team Murray (2009: 17) presents a strong case for diversity, stating that 'Diversity can add strength in complex situations if coupled with effective communication and positive relationships,' yet while team diversity is desirable, Field (2010) cautions against teams where a high incidence of diversity creates tensions and misunderstandings between colleagues. The balance and checks of team diversity are important, and can minimise conflict and confusion. Nowhere is this issue of greater priority as a quality assurance measure than in the area of child protection. Ample evidence exists from serious case reviews (Ofsted, 2009) indicating the need to ensure that communication channels, policies and procedures for safeguarding and protecting children are clear and unambiguous. More importantly, staff need to understand their role and obligations in protecting children and sharing information when there is a concern about a child. Ofsted (2009) has raised the importance of strong leadership to improve practice, and part of this requirement is the essential supervision of staff to monitor and improve professional practice.

Quality improvement – the case for supervision in early years

The concept and formality of professional or line management supervision may be alien in the early years sector; nonetheless, this aspect of professional practice merits consideration as a feature of quality improvement for services. There is ample and noteworthy emphasis on the importance of reflective practice for the EYP, and likewise the critical role of mentoring, a topic which receives sensitive and illuminative focus by Callan and Copp (2006).

There is a compelling case for supervision to be an additional responsibility for the early years manager, or an added dimension of the leadership role of the EYP (see Figure 8.1), as a quality improvement tool to protect and safeguard children. It is beyond the scope of this chapter to present and discuss the concept of supervision in any great depth, such as its many facets or protocols, the duty of care

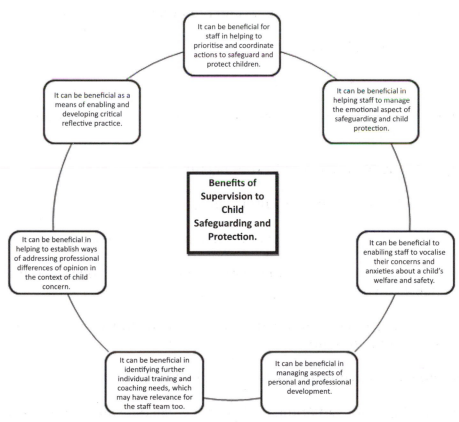

Figure 8.1 Some of the benefits of supervision in safeguarding children

to staff and how supervision systems can link with staff appraisals. The intention is to present the idea of supervision, and to consider the potential benefits of staff supervision as a quality assurance and service improvement measure.

Skills for Care (SfC) and Children's Workforce Development Council (CWDC) have jointly founded a supervision unit that is designed to promote a model of supervision for good practice and to assist in auditing and improving supervision where it occurs. When considering the introduction of supervision of staff, it would be a useful starting point to view the National Occupational Standards for Management and Leadership, which outlines the features of leadership and management of supervision for staff and the importance of planning and preparation for managers in their supervisory role (MSC, 2007). These standards provide some key indicators of good practice that underpin safeguarding and the supervision of staff, and include:

- managing your own resources and professional development;

- providing leadership in your team;

- managing risk;

- promoting equality of opportunity and diversity in your area of responsibility;

- encouraging innovation in your organisation;

- planning for and implementing change;

- developing productive working relationships with colleagues;

- developing productive working relationships with colleagues and stakeholders;

- allocating and monitoring the progress and quality of work in your area of responsibility;

- providing learning opportunities for colleagues;

- building and sustaining collaborative relationships with other organisations;

- ensuring that your own actions reduce risk to health and safety;

- ensuring that health and safety requirements are met in your area of responsibility;

- monitoring and solving customer service problems;

- working with others to improve customer service;

- managing quality audits.

Supervision may be defined as 'an accountable process which supports, assures and develops the knowledge, skills and values of an individual, group or team. The purpose is to improve the quality of their work to achieve agreed objectives and outcomes' (SfC and CWDC, 2007: 4). On considering some of the benefits of supervision to the workplace, Spouse and Redfern (2000) offer a helpful overview of the emergent themes of the process for the supervisor (the facilitator of supervision) and the supervisee (the active recipient). This is by no means a passive process and would require vested time and commitment from both the manager and the staff team, evolving as part of the ethos and culture of the early years setting. It is not, as Spouse and Redfern (2000: 7) suggest, 'simply a matter of a quick chat at six weekly intervals and a form being signed off'. The process is complex and demands two-way preparation from both parties, communicating reflective professional practice, professional development or practice concerns and improvements. It is an opportunity to acknowledge what is working well and to reflect and celebrate professional competence and skills. This mutuality of commitment and trust in the process seeks to ensure that it is a constructive and productive experience for the supervisee. There is a quality assurance outcome for the manager too, in having a better insight to the team and individual professional issues or concerns, which can impact on good practice in safeguarding and can be addressed at both individual and team levels.

Who should supervise who?

The provision of supervision should be available to all staff (paid and unpaid) within a setting, as a means of cementing team values and inclusivity. Spouse and Redfern (2000) highlight the importance of careful selection of who takes on the role of the supervisor; competence, confidence and expertise are essential prerequisites of the supervisor. It is worth considering that early years managers may not be best placed to assume this responsibility, due to other demands on their role. Arguably, it may be a responsibility for an EYP as an aspect of their leadership of good practice, where features of informing and educating staff go a long way to improving team practice and service delivery. Gray (2010) advocates the role of management within supervision but emphasises the proviso that the manager has the awareness and skill to be non-controlling, and can enable and empower staff in their development. If it is disempowering and controlling, staff may feel unsafe and less able to speak freely and confidently about raising their concerns or aspirations, and are likely to lose trust and engagement of the process.

Ethical matters

The safety net of good-quality supervision is another feature of quality improvement in safeguarding. Morrison (2005) refers to the requirement of a supervision contract, which highlights the mutual expectations and the establishment of a working agreement between supervisee and supervisor of this process. The formality of this contract should not be onerous but should serve as useful aide-mémoire or point of reference in working together, not unlike the agreement of ground rules within a training activity. The ethical considerations of the supervision process add an additional string to the bow of quality improvement. If the instrument is incomplete there can only be disharmony. It is necessary to understand the importance of confidentiality within the process of supervision and how this informs a colleague's training and development needs and their annual staff appraisal. There is an additional need for clear understanding between the supervisor and supervisee of the boundaries and limitations of confidentiality, and how information will be shared with early years managers as agreed and as appropriate, for example to support training needs or to feed into the appraisal process. The record of supervision in response to the agenda of supervision should be signed off and agreed by both parties, with a copy being presented to the supervisee for their records and future reference or follow-up action points. This supervision record should be treated as a confidential document and accessed only by the early years manager or others as agreed.

Supervision providing quality improvements in safeguarding and child protection

The professional constitution of the supervisor needs to be sound and fit for purpose and practice. Spouse and Redfern (2000: 8) suggest that 'supervision can be dangerous to self-esteem', as staff can be challenging of the stance of the supervisor or may not be open or receptive to challenge themselves, particularly when poor practice is observed as a concern. This is a critical issue and harks back to the earlier point of team diversity, which is healthy but must be in the right balance to prevent team conflicts, which may risk poor practice. The matter of strong opposing views of professional practice is not something to be shied away from, nor to be discouraged within the setting. It is a critical matter of how the dialogue occurs within the staff team; being encouraged to challenge the practice of each other as professionals is important, provided it occurs within the spirit of working effectively, respectfully and supportively together.

Dialogue and exchange of views are vital features of quality assurance; this is perhaps usefully illustrated in the case of child neglect. There may be some debate between an early years manager and a staff member about the threshold of intervention for other services. The early years practitioner might have observed the pattern of a child regularly turning up at the setting in a dirty and unfed state, sometimes with the mother and perhaps at other times with a man unknown as a family member. The debate is whether this picture would warrant a referral to Children's Social Care to register a concern. Efforts will have been made to discuss concerns with the child's mother, but she may have been elusive, avoiding contact with staff where possible. The opportunity to raise concerns about this child, particularly within the forum of supervision, can be very effective and reassuring to the practitioner and the supervisor. The outcome may pave a way forward to identify and address matters of inconsistent practice and ensuring better compliance with child protection policy and guidelines.

☐ **Summary**

The sensitive and astute leader is likely to appreciate that the prospect of supervision may be anxiety-provoking, and will require adequate reassurances and explanations. It is vital to see the provision of supervision as a feature of quality improvement in tandem with the mentoring processes within a team; both provisions should complement each other and demonstrate the true commitment to promoting better services to children and their families. Supervision is but one of the sturdy spokes emanating from the hub of a wheel of good-quality practice, forever in motion, with the child as centre focus. Ultimately, staff can take heart and have a degree of self-assurance that the need to be open and receptive to issues or concerns affecting the welfare of a child can be addressed through the mantle of supervision and ensuing professional dialogues within the setting.

References

AWCPP (2008) *All Wales Child Protection Procedures* (2nd edition). Wales: Local Safeguarding Board. Available at: http://www.ssiacymru.org.uk/media/pdf/0/4/Procedures.pdf (last accessed 2 December 2010).

Callan, S. and Copp, E. (2006) 'The mentor as "the one in the middle"', in A. Robins (ed.), *Mentoring in the Early Years*. London: Paul Chapman Publishing.

Cleaver, H., Unell, I. and Aldgate, J. (1999) *Children's Needs – Parenting Capacity. The Impact of Parental Mental Illness, Problem Alcohol and Drug Use, and Domestic Violence on Children's Development*. London: The Stationary Office.

Department for Children, Schools and Families (DCSF) (2009) *Think Family Toolkit: Improving Support for Families at Risk*. Nottingham: DCSF.

Department for Children, Schools and Families (DCSF) (2010) *Working Together to Safeguard Children* (updated version). Nottingham: DCSF.

Department for Education and Skills (DfES) (2006) *Working Together to Safeguard Children*. London: The Stationery Office.

Field, R. (2010) 'Self-awareness and leadership', in I. Gray, R. Field and K. Brown (eds), *Effective Leadership, Management and Supervision in Health and Social Care*. Exeter: Learning Matters.

Gardner, R. and Cleaver, H. (2009) 'Working effectively with parents', in H. Cleaver, P. Cawson, S. Gorin and S. Walker (eds), *Safeguarding Children: A Shared Responsibility*. Chichester: Wiley-Blackwell.

Goleman, D. (1998) *Working with Emotional Intelligence*. London: Bloomsbury.

Gray, I. (2010) 'The role and importance of supervision', in I. Gray, R. Field and K. Brown (eds), *Effective Leadership, Management and Supervision in Health and Social Care*. Exeter: Learning Matters.

Gupta, A. (2010) 'We must strive to understand the complex lives of children', *The Guardian*, 10 March, p. 3.

Haringey Local Safeguarding Children Board (LSCB) (2009) *Serious Case Review: Baby Peter. Executive Summary*. London: Haringey Council.

Jones, D. (2001) 'The assessment of parental capacity', in J. Horwath (ed.), *The Child's World*. London: Jessica Kingsley.

Management Standards Centre (MSC) (2007) *National Occupational Standards for Management and Leadership*. London: Chartered Management Institute.

Morrison, T. (2005) *Strength to Strength: A Facilitator's Guide to Preparing Supervisees, Students and Trainees for Supervision*. Brighton: Pavilion Publishing.

Munro, E. (2008) *Effective Child Protection* (2nd edition). London: Sage.

Munro, E. (2010) *The Munro Review of Child Protection, Part One: A Systems Analysis*. London: Department for Education.

Murray, J. (2009) 'Value-based leadership and management', in A. Robins and S. Callan (eds), *Managing Early Years Settings*. London: Sage.

Ofsted (2009) *Learning Lessons from Serious Case Reviews: Year 2*. Manchester: Ofsted.

Pilcher, M. (2009) 'Making a positive contribution', in A. Robins and S. Callan (eds), *Managing Early Years Settings*. London: Sage.

Quinton, D. (2004) *Supporting Parents: Messages for Research*. London: Jessica Kingsley.

Richards, C. (2010) 'Safeguarding children: Every Child Matters so everybody matters!', in M. Reed and N. Canning (eds), *Reflective Practice in the Early Years*. London: Sage.

Skills for Care (SfC) and Children's Workforce Development Council (CWDC) (2007) *Providing Effective Supervision*. Leeds: Skills for Care.

Spouse, J. and Redfern, L. (2000) 'Creating a quality service', in J. Spouse and L. Redfern (eds), *Successful Supervision in Health Care Practice*. Oxford: Blackwell Science.

9

'Go softly . . .': the reality of 'leading practice' in early years settings

Rory McDowall Clark and Sue Baylis

Chapter overview

This chapter considers the crucial role of effective leadership as a determinant of quality provision. The link between leaders with higher qualifications and improved outcomes for young children is now undisputed (Muijs et al., 2004; Siraj-Blatchford and Manni, 2007; Dunlop, 2008) and underpins the drive towards professionalising the early years workforce (McDowall Clark and Baylis, 2010). The establishment of Early Years Professional Status (EYPS) in England recognised the importance of skilled graduate practitioners and their impact on pedagogy, the quality of curriculum experiences and relationships that are the basis of children's learning and development. However, EYPS is still establishing itself and uncertainty remains about EYPs' role in leading practice and how this differs from conventional ideas of leadership associated with management. This chapter explores the reality of 'leading practice' and the strategies employed by EYPs in improving provision and contributing to quality. A model of catalytic leadership (McDowall Clark, 2010a) is discussed which argues that professionals' ability to bring about quality improvement from within their settings is not dependent on holding a position of power.

The link between quality and qualifications

The first decade of the twenty-first century saw unprecedented attention paid to the early years, with massive investment in the sector by the New Labour government (1997–2010). Although early years provision is usually considered a service for young children, it is important to remember that childcare actually serves a wider political agenda in also supporting the economy and employment (McDowall Clark, 2010b). Therefore the need to extend and develop provision may be at odds with the drive to improve quality. In particular, the growth of the private sector raises concerns about the need for profitability (Penn, 2007). Measures to address these concerns resulted in a new registration and inspection framework under Ofsted, the introduction of a single curricular framework for 0–5 age range in the Early Years Foundation Stage (DCSF, 2008) and development of Early Years Professionals (EYPs) to lead practice and act as change agents (CWDC, 2010). This last move was particularly important because it represented the long overdue professionalisation of the early years workforce (McDowall Clark and Baylis, 2010). However, although Muijs et al. (2004) identified leadership as a key element of quality in early years settings, many EYPs working in positions that lack the authority of management felt anxious about the expectations laid on them and insecure in their ability to lead practice.

The connection between graduate practitioners and quality, first made in the Rumbold Report, *Starting with Quality* (DES, 1990) and reinforced by the *Start Right* report (Ball, 1994), led to the establishment of Early Childhood Studies degrees, now prolific throughout the UK. However, it took another decade and a change of government before investment in graduate professionals became part of official policy. *Choice for Parents*, a ten year strategy laying out a long-term vision for universal provision in the UK, recognised that 'the single biggest factor that determines the quality of childcare is the workforce' (HM Treasury, 2004: 44). The impetus driving this was the evidence base from the longitudinal EPPE research study (Effective Provision of Pre-school Education) project in England (Sylva et al., 2004). EPPE concluded that high-quality early years provision not only has lasting effects on children's development but also helps reduce consequences of social disadvantage. Later extended to follow children into primary and secondary school, EPPE has impacted on all areas of early years provision and policy by identifying factors that make a difference to outcomes for children. Key among these was the presence of graduate staff and this finding informed the Children's Workforce Strategy

(DfES, 2006b), charged with upskilling the large workforce employed in the sector.

Most of the evidence from EPPE focused on the contribution of trained teachers because this comprised the majority of graduates in the study, so one of the possibilities considered was the introduction of early years qualified teachers into settings. However, the approach eventually selected was a social pedagogue model such as is common in Scandinavian countries. This accentuates the integrated and holistic nature of the early years sector rather than laying the stress on teaching. Resistance to the term 'pedagogue' led to the name Early Years Professional being adopted for a new graduate role charged with leading practice to improve quality. As Cameron (2004: 19) points out, 'the essential point is to lift working with children out of a series of task-based occupations and towards the idea of a critical thinking, creative, team working professional'. An additional hope is that improving the status of working in the early years should eventually impact on pay and conditions, thus helping to retain high-calibre staff within the sector.

Perspectives of leadership

Traditional theories of leadership have been based on hierarchical models because they are adapted from business practices that do not transfer well to the early years sector. Despite the need to be financially viable, the core activity of early years settings is founded on a value base rather than a profit motive, so conventional hierarchies that take a top-down approach can be in conflict with the early years ethos. An alternative, less hierarchical understanding of leadership is one that suggests progress and advance towards a goal. Rather than being structural, this type of transformational or visionary leadership (Avery, 2004) focuses on individual interpersonal skills to inspire and support others. This is more likely to be found in early years settings where even if a leader is nominally in charge they may prefer to adopt a 'flatter', more democratic style of leadership, treating other workers as colleagues rather than subordinates and 'cultivating a valuing culture' (Canning, 2009: 26).

Rodd (2006: 16) points out that many early years professionals are 'averse to being in a position of dominance' so the second model in Figure 9.1, moving away from giving direct orders to more subtle encouragement, leading from the front may appear more appealing and 'human'. However, both models nevertheless imply

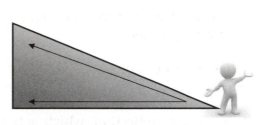

Leadership from above   Leadership from in front

Figure 9.1 Models of leadership

power, whether this is positional or personal. They are based on the established notion of a leader being 'in charge' or at least in a position of authority. This assumption shapes most people's view of leadership.

Leadership in the early years

In recent years a growing focus on early years leadership has resulted in a number of texts exploring leadership as a concept and attempting to identify particular skills and attributes of leaders (for example, Moyles, 2004; Rodd, 2006; Aubrey, 2007; Callan and Robins, 2009). This development has been fuelled by the recognition that 'there is a significant relationship between the qualities of a setting and its leadership' (Murray et al., 2009: 2). However, the increase of literature exploring leadership also causes problems for practitioners in the field because of the many different approaches and interpretations of the term. In particular leadership and management are usually discussed together as if they are the same thing, and because 'the complementary nature of leadership and management is often assumed' (Dunlop, 2008: 4) there is also a supposition that leadership is necessarily connected with authority and power. This means that the focus of investigation is primarily on managerial leadership.

One of the most influential studies of early years leadership is the ELEYS Study in England (Effective Leadership in the Early Years Sector) (Siraj-Blatchford and Manni, 2007). This set out to discover characteristics of leadership displayed in settings providing effective pedagogy (Siraj-Blatchford et al., 2002). The following categories of effective practice were identified:

- identifying and articulating a collective vision, especially with regard to pedagogy and curriculum;

- ensuring shared understandings, meanings and goals, building common purposes;

- effective communication, providing a level of *transparency* in regard to expectations, practices and processes;

- encouraging reflection, which acts as an impetus for change and the motivation for ongoing learning and development;

- commitment to ongoing, professional development, supporting staff to become more critically reflective in their practice;

- monitoring and assessing practice, through collaborative dialogue and action research;

- building a learning community and team culture, establishing a community of learners;

- encouraging and facilitating parent and community partnerships, promoting achievement for all young children.

Siraj-Blatchford and Manni (2007: 27) focus specifically on managerial leaders, drawing attention to how it is 'necessary to reconcile the sometimes competing demands of leadership and management'. However, management and leadership are separate, distinct functions. The task of management is concerned with day-to-day operations, ensuring that an organisation runs smoothly, whereas leadership entails responsibility for motivation and development towards a shared vision. The establishment of EYPS creates a new expectation: that of modelling and leading *practice*. This pedagogic leadership is quite different from traditional organisational leadership, although within small settings one person may undertake both roles. For many EYPs this is indeed the case – they are managers or deputies of settings, children's centre teachers or others whose role clearly identifies a certain degree of weight and influence. However, there are a considerable number of EYPs whose position is much more ambiguous. They may be young graduates working within teams of older, more experienced but lesser qualified practitioners; possibly they are the only person in the setting with a degree and therefore selected to become the EYP; or they may be someone whose enthusiasm about their own personal continuing professional development (CPD) has led them to pursue a Foundation Degree. Such people are often less confident about their role as leaders and can find it difficult to recognise their own part in bringing about change. Avery (2004) suggests that most people, unprompted, will cling to a concept of 'control and command' leadership and this undermines both EYPs' own view of their influence and often that of other people they work with.

Leading practice from within

Part of the role of EYPS providers is to support candidates in exploring and articulating their own leadership and to consider how they lead practice within their settings. Traditional ideas about leaders directing the actions of others have prevented many from recognising their own practice as leadership; however, opportunities to discuss and share experiences have enabled EYPs to review and revise their concepts of a leader. In the following examples and case studies, the names and identifying details have been changed to ensure anonymity for individuals and their settings.

A joint exploration can provoke new ways of envisioning leadership in which the EYP acts as a catalyst within their setting (McDowall Clark, 2010a). A catalyst is a substance which when added to a mixture brings about internal change to create something new. This model of *catalytic leadership* challenges the view that leadership comes from 'above' or 'in front'. Thus an EYP can lead practice from anywhere within an organisation. The aversion to dominance identified by Rodd (2006) is evident in the low-key, sensitive manner in which EYPS candidates choose to lead practice, as this group identified:

> *Sandy*: It's about . . . being *part* of change and not dictating what that change is. It shows other staff that you're inclusive.
> *Katy*: Yes. Collaboration is so important for everything. You can't just march in . . .
> *Abbi*: [*laughing*] Well, you *can* do, but . . .
> *Sandy*: Yes, you can, but it's not going to work.

This demonstrates professionals' awareness of the need to take others with them and that confrontation is unlikely to be the best way to bring about change. Such discussions brought to light many unobtrusive and inconspicuous ways in which EYPs extend and develop the understanding of others. The following is an example of how Sally achieved this in her setting.

Case study 1: Sally

Sally graduated three years ago and works with a number of older practitioners, who while not overtly negative are not in the habit of reflecting on practice. As a result they are quite happy to continue to work in the ways they are used to and see no need for change.

One practitioner, Margaret, spent a morning assessing the children's number and colour recognition through an activity she had devised that involved cutting and sticking shapes to make a car (linked to the current 'transport' theme). Later she mentioned to Sally her concern that little Daisy could hardly count and did not know any of her colours.

The next day Sally saw Daisy sitting at the mark-making table and went and sat down next to her. She began to draw and casually engaged Daisy in conversation. Sally asked her if she would pass the blue crayon, commented that green was her favourite colour and asked Daisy what her favourite colour was?' Sally realised that in fact Daisy was aware of all the colours and could count quite competently up to 7. She casually mentioned her experience to Margaret, adding in puzzlement, 'I wonder why she couldn't do it yesterday?' Margaret suggested that perhaps her activity had been too structured and formal and might not have been the most appropriate way to assess Daisy's true abilities.

In this case study Sally is very effective in leading practice even though she is not in a position of authority over other practitioners. It would be unfair to accuse Margaret of bad practice; it is evident that she is avoiding testing the children and has carefully planned an activity that she hopes will be meaningful to them. However, Sally recognises that it is very adult-directed and certainly not the most effective way of assessing their abilities. Rather than overtly challenging Margaret's activity, which could make her defensive, Sally asks questions that prompt her to rethink her approach. Such a tactic can be argued to be a more effective way of bringing about change and enhancing practice than outright confrontation. Sally has recognised that genuine improvement can only come about if Margaret becomes aware of issues for herself. Reflection on practice is an essential component of quality improvement (Appleby, 2010; also see Michael Reed, Chapter 1; and Karen Appleby and Mandy Andrews, Chapter 4) and Sally actively models a reflective approach by speculating, 'I wonder why she couldn't do it yesterday?' This strategy of making reflection visible by talking through practice and evaluating 'out loud' is a key aspect of catalytic leadership.

A common concern for many is the fact that change is a slow process and it cannot be accomplished overnight. A realistic and sensible approach is to look for ways of enhancing quality that are achievable and build on opportunities available rather than try to bring about sweeping change that makes others feel intimidated or insecure. Payler and Locke (2010) point out that experienced early years staff, who have endured low pay with high levels of commitment for years, need to feel that they *own* the changes.

Many EYPs recognise that beginning with those members of staff who are receptive to change can be more successful than trying to change mindsets and attitudes of those who are resistant. For instance Esther (see below), who lacked support in challenging the ethos and accepted practice within her setting, recommended: 'It's more effective to work with a few people because when they pick up on what you are trying to change it has more effect – a double knock-on effect!'

Case study 2: Esther

Esther was concerned that behaviour management in her nursery was frequently inappropriate to children's development and level of understanding. She found it challenging to make a difference in this area without the support of colleagues and therefore concentrated her efforts on working with individual practitioners who seemed the most receptive to change.

Esther had observed that two-year-old Jamie was struggling to make friends and his attempts to relate to other children often resulted in aggression. One day he was shouted at by Sheila, one of the practitioners, for biting another child. Engaging Sheila in conversation, Esther wondered whether shouting was the best way to deal with the problem and suggested that perhaps Jamie needed support with his social development. Sheila asked Esther to suggest other ways to deal with such outbursts and Esther modelled playing alongside Jamie, helping him to interact with other children and giving him lots of praise and encouragement. However, Sheila was unhappy with this approach; she felt that Jamie was 'getting away with biting' as he had not been punished.

A few days later a group of practitioners were discussing the bad behaviour of a child in another room where the practitioner had lost her temper. Both Esther and Sheila were present and Esther talked again about appropriate ways to encourage children's positive behaviour and mentioned the problems Jamie was experiencing. The following day she was delighted to see Sheila sitting on the floor with the boy and supporting him in interacting with other children. She hopes that Sheila's example alongside her own will now be effective in helping to challenge unthinking practice.

Here Esther takes a similar approach to that of Sally in the previous case study, by raising questions and making reflection explicit. Her support of her colleague is tactful, enabling Sheila to admit to difficulties in managing Jamie's behaviour. Esther sets an example by modelling good practice, explaining her rationale and how this will be more effective in supporting Jamie. Although Sheila is not initially convinced she is able to mull over Esther's different approach; seeing another practitioner reacting inappropriately later enables her to revise her own response.

Leading practice and bringing about positive change is often a matter of sowing seeds in this way. They may not take root immediately but this should not discourage EYPs from continuing to model high principles and expectations. Long-term quality improvement requires genuine conviction on the part of practitioners rather than the short-term change resulting from obedient compliance. A leader with authority conferred by a job title can impose change through power invested in their role; but a catalytic leader brings about change in other ways. This change is 'progressive rather than being achieved by a single action or characteristic' (Canning, 2009: 27). Both Margaret and Sheila were encouraged to reflect on their practice by EYP colleagues in a way that ensured that any change in their approach would be genuine. This should have a long-term effect on their practice and so continue to improve the quality of provision.

Barriers and constraints

The leadership of practice discussed so far stems to a great extent from EYPs' huge enthusiasm about their own professional development. Those who have taken Foundation Degrees as a precursor to EYPS talk about how this 'opened up a real thirst for learning', and they would like to promote a similar outlook among colleagues. For instance, Lynn says: 'I want to encourage the attitude that learning always occurs even after qualifications are gained.' She is trying to develop a culture of learning so that practitioners feel empowered to improve and develop practice themselves. This kind of community of practice (Wenger, 1998) is important for quality improvement but not always easy to achieve. Staff who do not want to 'progress' or feel anxious about their ability to match up to expectations may see little point in ongoing professional development. Sian notes: 'there are some members of staff who give the impression they have little time for higher qualifications so I am working slowly and carefully to change the mindset.' One of the ways EYPs work to 'change this mindset' and establish a community of practice is through modelling reflection, as we have already considered. Another is by recognising and supporting colleagues' individual strengths so that they can be given ownership of particular aspects of practice. Without this commitment and interest then other practitioners may prefer to avoid the risks of responsibility.

📁 Case study 3: Annie

Annie is currently the only practitioner with a qualification above level 3 in her setting. While studying for her degree Annie became very interested in outdoor play and has gradually worked to develop the outside provision at her setting. In particular she was keen to utilise a number of trees, which offer lots of opportunities for climbing. Staff were originally very anxious about allowing children to climb trees, but Annie discussed the benefits of appropriate risk-taking in staff meetings. She put together a folder of information from her research and developed suitable risk assessments. Now, other members of staff are prepared to allow the children to climb trees when Annie is present, 'because Annie says they're allowed to'. Annie would like other practitioners to recognise for themselves how the children's experiences outside can be extended, rather than need somebody to tell them what to do. She feels that in 'solving' the issue of climbing trees she has uncovered another, deeper problem.

Annie's impact on practice in her setting is clear; she has extended the use of the outdoors considerably and taken opportunities to share her knowledge and enthusiasm with colleagues. However, further improvement is being undermined by the staff's limited pedagogical understanding and reluctance to take on responsibility themselves. Annie can continue to move practice forward step by step but there is a danger that this may be misinterpreted or only understood on a superficial level with 'some practitioners . . . not seeing beyond the "activity idea" when observing modelled practice' (Garrick and Morgan, 2009: 76).

Working to establish a culture in which critical enquiry and dialogue can flourish takes time. The PVI (private, voluntary and independent) sector in particular is vulnerable to 'limiting factors' such as low pay and poor working conditions, which can result in unskilled, uncommitted employees. Garrick and Morgan (2009) suggest that if these

conditions persist they are likely to prevent the potential of committed pedagogical leaders such as EYPs from being fully realised.

A model of catalytic leadership

It is evident that leadership within early years differs in many
fundamental ways from leadership in other areas, even within the
field of education. In particular, the sector is unique in identifying
a role for leaders of practice as distinct from leaders of provision. For
EYPs who are expected to lead practice from 'within' this may require
a major shift in their understanding of what a leader does. The concept
of catalytic leadership (McDowall Clark, 2010a) offers a model that is
more appropriate to leaders of practice and fits alongside the ethos and
philosophy of the early years. This is a relatively informal leadership
in which change emerges rather than is imposed (see Figure 9.2).

An EYP acting as a catalyst within their setting does not necessarily
have the power to enforce sweeping changes, and therefore they work
from a position of influence rather than authority. They recognise that
this can be effective in terms of lasting quality improvement, which
requires practitioners to be committed to change and not simply
comply because they must. A catalytic leader recognises potential
and possibilities and works to bring about long-term change through
small, incremental steps. In this way it can be seen that catalytic
leadership is a creative, dynamic process rather than a set of attitudes
or behaviours.

The role of EYPs as graduate professionals charged with leading
practice is still in its early stages and Whalley (2008: 9) points out the
need to define a new model of leadership for this status, suggesting
that it must 'fit across all types of early years settings and sit equally
comfortably in a home setting, a voluntary pre-school in a small
village school, a private nursery or a large children's centre'. The model
of catalytic leadership can do this while at the same time meeting
the criteria for effective leadership identified by Siraj-Blatchford and
Manni (2007). It is also a model that empowers EYPs by enabling
them to recognise their own potential for bringing about quality
improvement regardless of their position within an organisation.

The assumption that leadership depends on power and is about
directing others' practice initially prevented many EYPs from
recognising their own leadership potential. Some admitted that
they had not previously thought of themselves as leaders and were

Small steps and
incremental
changes

Supportive, non-
confrontational
challenge

Commitment to
professional
development

Reflective
practice making
pedagogy explicit

Figure 9.2 Catalytic leadership

concerned about how they might demonstrate leadership of practice without a position of authority to legitimise their ideas. This can be a particular issue for those who work independently, such as Lisa, an activities worker in a children's centre. Lisa's job was a new post and so she had created her role from scratch, developing provision in a fixed building as well as within the wider community. She played an important part in her team and had established good links with teachers, midwives, family support workers and others throughout the neighbourhood. Lisa was concerned to model good practice, openly reflecting and encouraging others to do so too. However, she initially struggled to see the leadership inherent in her role because she was not in a position of directly supervising others. Opportunities to discuss and reflect on their individual roles and approaches have prompted new EYPs such as Lisa to identify the ways they influence and improve practice within their own settings. The process has also helped to validate EYP's own self-belief in their ability to make a difference and promote their confidence as change agents (CWDC, 2010). For genuine quality improvement to become embedded in early years practice it is crucial that EYPs play a strong role in its design and development, commensurate with their professional status.

Maintaining quality for the future

This chapter has discussed 'quality' as if it represents an objective statement of fact that is universal and measurable. Policy measures to improve and uphold quality certainly take this approach, and Dahlberg and Moss (2005) warn that often quality is about establishing conformity to predetermined standards. As increasing measures are brought in to ensure quality provision, early years practitioners are accountable to a wide range of stakeholders, including parents and carers, the community, local authorities and government officials, as well as children themselves. This is a serious responsibility and requires reflective and questioning professionals to be prepared to engage with the philosophical and ethical issues entailed in the quest for quality (Dahlberg et al., 2002). EYPs must be prepared to take on this challenge if quality improvement is to be more than a technical exercise.

The unprecedented focus on the early years, with subsequent investment and commitment to development, was instigated by the Labour government (1997–2010). The Childcare Act (DfES, 2006a) requires local authorities to improve outcomes for all young children and reduce inequalities between them; this expectation is dependent on high-quality provision supported by a skilled professional workforce. It is difficult (at a time of cuts in public funding and service budgets) to see how these two agendas might be reconciled. Siraj-Blatchford and Manni (2007: 11) point out how the disparities between publicly funded provision and the private sector are obstacles to change. They suggest that 'it is difficult to see how more qualified early years staff will be remunerated for their continued training or how retention can be improved in some sectors without improving pay'. This is a concern because the 'limiting factors' affecting the impact of those leading practice in the PVI sector is a real impediment to improving quality (Garrick and Morgan, 2009). As Dunlop (2008: 16) recognises, 'a political commitment or culture is required, so creating the opportunity for improvement in the quality of early childhood services as newly trained leaders become agents for change'.

Summary

The growth of accountability and the drive for high-quality provision to improve outcomes for young children has led to an increasing emphasis on strong leadership within the early years sector. However, the corresponding literature focuses primarily on managerial leadership and assumes that leaders have the power to tell others what to do. Consequently, unexamined assumptions and limited interpretation of leadership can make it difficult for those who do not have a managerial role or a position of authority from which to influence and instigate good practice. Early Years Professionals in such situations may initially lack confidence or awareness of their own opportunity to make a difference and need encouragement to recognise how they lead practice and support others. The model of catalytic leadership, whereby EYPs bring about change through influence rather than power, is helpful in contextualising how quality improvement can happen from within. Catalytic leaders make their pedagogy explicit and model reflective practice to others. As catalysts within their settings, EYPs introduce small changes that challenge others' thinking rather than criticise their practice. This is a starting point for developing a culture of life-learning and can help to establish reflective communities of practice (Wenger, 1998). EYPs are a key part of quality implementation and they need to have a corresponding professional voice appropriate to the professionalism they are expected to observe.

References

Appleby, K. (2010) 'Reflective thinking, reflective practice', in M. Reed and N. Canning (eds), *Reflective Practice in the Early Years*. London: Sage.

Aubrey, C. (2007) *Leading and Managing in the Early Years*. London: Sage.

Avery, G. (2004) *Understanding Leadership: Paradigms and Cases*. London: Sage.

Ball, C. (1994) *Start Right: The Importance of Early Learning*. London: Royal Society of Arts.

Callan, S. and Robins, A. (eds) (2009) *Managing and Leading in the Early Years*. London: Sage.

Cameron, C. (2004) *Building an Integrated Workforce for a Long-term Vision of Universal Early Education and Care*. London: Day Care Trust.

Canning, N. (2009) 'Empowering communities through inspirational leadership', in A. Robins and S. Callan (eds), *Managing Early Years Settings*. London: Sage.

Children's Workforce Development Council (CWDC) (2010) *Early Years Professional Status*. Available at: http://www.cwdcouncil.org.uk/eyps (last accessed 4 October 2010).

Dahlberg, G. and Moss, P. (2005) *Ethics and Politics in Early Childhood Education*. London: Routledge Falmer,

Dahlberg, G., Moss, P. and Pence, A. (2002) *Beyond Quality in Early Childhood Education and Care*. London: Routledge Falmer.

Department for Children, Schools and Families (DCSF) (2008) *The Early Years Foundation Stage*. Nottingham: DCSF.

Department for Education and Skills (DfES) (2006a) *The Childcare Act 2006*. London: DfES.

Department for Education and Skills (DfES) (2006b) *Children's Workforce Strategy: Building on Integrated Qualifications Framework*. London: DfES.

Department of Education and Science (DES) (1990) *Starting with Quality: Report of the Committee of Enquiry into the Quality of Educational Experience Offered to Three and Four Year Olds (Rumbold Report)*. London: DES/HMSO.

Dunlop, A.W. (2008) *A Literature Review on Leadership in the Early Years*. Dundee: Learning and Teaching Scotland.

Garrick, R. and Morgan, A. (2009) 'The children's centre teacher role: developing practice in the private, voluntary and independent sector', *Early Years*, 29 (1): 69–81.

HM Treasury (2004) *Choice for Parents, the Best Start for Children: A Ten Year Strategy for Children*. London: HMSO.

McDowall Clark, R. (2010a) '"I'd never thought of myself as a leader . . .": reconceptualising leadership with early years professionals', conference paper, 20th EECERA Conference, Birmingham, 6–8 September.

McDowall Clark, R. (2010b) *Childhood in Society for Early Childhood Studies*. Exeter: Learning Matters.

McDowall Clark, R. and Baylis, S. (2010) 'The new professionals: leading for change', in M. Reed and N. Canning (eds), *Reflective Practice in the Early Years*. London: Sage.

Moyles, J. (2004) *Effective Leadership and Management in the Early Years*. Maidenhead: Open University Press.

Muijs, D., Aubrey, C., Harris A. and Briggs, M. (2004) 'How do they manage? A review of the research on leadership in early childhood', *Journal of Early Childhood Research*, 2 (2): 157–69.

Murray, J., Robins, A. and Callan, S. (2009) 'Introduction', in A. Robins and S. Callan (eds), *Managing Early Years Settings*. London: Sage.

Payler, J. and Locke, R. (2010) 'Disrupting communities of practice? Practitioners' views on the introduction of Early Years Professional Status', conference paper, Early Childhood Curriculum, Policy and Pedagogy in the 21st Century: An International Debate, Anglia Ruskin University, 25–27 March.

Penn, H. (2007) 'Childcare market management: how the United Kingdom government has reshaped its role in developing early childhood education and care', *Contemporary Issues in the Early Years*, 8 (3): 192–207.

Rodd, J. (2006) *Leadership in Early Childhood* (3rd edition). Maidenhead: Open University Press.

Siraj-Blatchford, I. and Manni, L. (2007) *Effective Leadership in the Early Years Sector (ELEYS) Study – Research Report*. London: Institute of Education, University of London/General Teaching Council for England.

Siraj-Blatchford, I., Sylva, K., Muttock, S., Gilden, R. and Bell, D. (2002) *Researching Effective Pedagogy in the Early Years (REPEY)*, DfES Research Report 356. London: DfES/HMSO.

Sylva, K., Melhuish, E.C., Sammons, P., Siraj-Blatchford I. and Taggart, B. (2004)

The Effective Provision of Pre-School Education (EPPE) Project: Final Report. London: DfES/Institute of Education, University of London.

Wenger, E. (1998) *Communities of Practice: Learning, Meaning and Identity.* Cambridge: Cambridge University Press.

Whalley, M.E. (2008) *Leading Practice in Early Years Settings.* Exeter: Learning Matters.

10

Parents and practitioners: improving quality

Michael Reed and Alison Murphy

Chapter overview

This chapter considers the value of collaboration between mothers, fathers, carers and early years services. It suggests that such collaboration is an essential part of quality improvement and that parents themselves are an essential part of developing quality practice. It introduces a selection of evidence, taken from the wealth of material that exists about the subject. This evidence underpins the value of parental intervention and considers key aspects about what promotes quality 'partnership programmes' and support in the community.

There is a significant volume of literature about what constitutes 'quality' in early years settings. This has tended to focus on professional definitions of quality rather than parental perspectives on quality. So we start by reminding ourselves what Rhodes (2008) asks us, which is to 'think child' when trying to understand families and to welcome the diversity we find in families. This is important because there is considerable evidence that shows the importance of positive parenting on children's development and how when this is combined with professional involvement it has a powerful effect on children's learning. What is more, this seems to be true even when other factors, such as the effect of poor attainment or social class, have been factored out and relies mostly on positive attitudes, values and aspirations which support children's learning (Desforges and Abouchaar, 2003). There is also evidence from Wheeler et al. (2009), who note the powerful effect of home and family for children's social and intellectual development, and suggest the most effective early years settings work closely with parents.

Having parents working with practitioners really does make a difference and can raise achievement (Harris et al., 2009). Parents should be consulted and listened to about their children's care and education and asked about what is important to them in terms of quality early years provision. Jackson (2010) posed this question to parents and found that the response was an individualised perspective. We suspect that this is because any parental determination of quality will be based upon personal experiences. It will be dependent upon a parent's experience of the care shown to their child or their experience in accessing services or the way professionals have acted towards them. A parent's response will also be influenced by the way they as children and adults came into contact with early years practitioners and the influence of government policies and local resources. It will be seen in terms of the way people are treated, the way early years practitioners provide 'rights' for children and the way they protect children from harm. We should also remember that we operate in a socio-political world which impacts on people's views about work, childhood and the quality of care (Baldock et al., 2009).

All these factors may influence views expressed about quality but it will not make them any less valid or important, sometimes just different. We therefore need to understand what we mean by 'parents and carers' in today's world, because families are not static or remain the same. Society changes, economic factors change and the way we live and work has changed. The Green Paper *Support for All: Families and Relationships* (DCSF, 2010d), presented to Parliament January 2010, stated that in 2008, 64 per cent of children were living in families with married couples, 23 per cent of children lived with a lone parent and 13 per cent lived with co-habiting couples, which covers a wide range of relationships, including those that lead to marriage and those that do not. Marriage rates appear to be declining since their peak in the 1970s and in general, women are having fewer children and doing so later in life. However, right across Europe the proportion of children born outside marriage has increased very significantly, and there is greater acceptance and recognition of same-sex relationships including formal partnerships. The majority of grandparents now see their grandchildren grow up because people are living longer. There is an increased range of opportunities being enjoyed by young women from families on middle and higher incomes. However, there are limited opportunities for teenage mothers who live in deprived areas (DCSF, 2010d).

There are also varied views on childcare. Over half (58 per cent) of working mothers took advantage of 'informal' childcare such as grandparents. In most cases the affordability and quality of childcare remained positive, but a quarter of mothers reported that there was limited access to early years settings and it was not considered affordable. Parents were generally positive about the quality of childcare, with over half saying that it was 'very' or 'fairly' good (Maplethorpe et al., 2010). Of course, this is only a snapshot of what is occurring today and we make no predictions for the future based upon this evidence. However, it reinforces the need to examine and interrogate changes in the social context in which we work. The Green Paper (DCSF, 2010d: 5) goes on to say that the 'sheer diversity of family life now rules out "one size fits all" approaches'. Interestingly, from a professional perspective, it suggests that 'giving families access to information, advice and support of various kinds that they can use as and when they think best is much more likely to be effective'. This is an important comment and means that early years practitioners should recognise the diversity of family life and embrace changing practices as well as the growing influence of digital and other technology that informs, educates and makes communication between sections of society almost instant.

These developments may influence policy-makers; however, collaboration and partnership with parents still rests with the day-to-day work of practitioners. It is they who are the implementers of quality services and who provide a consistent approach to supporting parents' needs. It is this consistency and responsiveness that is so important and the bedrock of quality. This view may appear simplistic and one that has probably been articulated many times before; nevertheless, it is important to recognise the part played by individual professionals in determining the quality of support a parent receives. This is well documented in relation to support for families with children who have additional needs (Hodge and Runswick-Cole, 2008). They suggest it is those professionals who are willing to learn about the *child* who provide positive support, rather than those who want to know only about the disability. This view tells us that placing the child at the centre of what we do should always be our priority. Sometimes this may not be easy, but it is very important in the context of parental intervention and support.

Parental partnership: some driving forces

In considering parental partnerships we should look towards the curriculum frameworks in the UK. They consist of the following:

- Wales – Foundation Phase for children's learning, 3–7 years (DCELLS, 2008)

- Northern Ireland – Curricular Guidance for Pre-school Education (DENI, 2008)

- England – Early Years Foundation Stage (DCSF, 2008)

- Scotland – Curriculum for Excellence for children and young people aged 3 to 18 (Scottish Government 2008; Kidner, 2010)

These frameworks contain requirements, directives, suggestions and advice that underline the importance of collaboration and positive information exchange with parents. Parental partnership is therefore an integrated feature of curriculum frameworks and forms part of the inspection process in the nations of the UK. It is also a significant focus of the Quality Improvement Principles (NQIN, 2007). In practice, this means that we are asked to take steps to help children learn while acknowledging the different situations and contexts, including the home, which may impact on their learning. All this is built upon an increasing emphasis to improve practitioner and parental partnerships (LPPA, 2010). It is becoming clear that practitioners today are required to understand much more about the influence of the family in shaping children's experiences. This may lead towards what Moss et al. (2007) see as a desire to forge an active participation within communities and between practitioners and parents to understand and support children's play and learning processes. Gasper (2010) acknowledges this as a change in philosophy and action towards community support. As for the benefits on children's well-being when practitioners and families work as an effective team, there is now a body of research that acknowledges the importance of such collaboration.

Desforges and Abouchaar (2003) suggest that what parents 'do' with their children is highly significant in terms of a child's development, education and emotional well-being. They argue that this is not limited to planned activities, outings or new experiences but involves everyday engagement and interaction. These experiences may seem mundane or routine, but they should not be taken for granted and are of singular importance to the child. Indeed, research has shown that young children achieve more and are happier when practitioners work together with parents and share ideas about how to support and extend children's learning (Athey, 1990; Meade, 1995). Parents are now encouraged to spend time playing with their children and asked to see their role as responding to their child's preferred style of learning (Reed and Walker, 2011). As for the long-term benefits of parental partnerships, Desforges and Abouchaar (2003: 91) review the subject and suggest that we look carefully at what works 'not just from the perspective of research and longitudinal studies, but also alongside the work and views of practitioners themselves'. This is something highlighted in the DCSF report *Breaking the Link Between Disadvantage and Low Achievement in the Early Years* (2010a). The report contains examples of practice and an overview of research evidence, and makes clear the need to support and engage with disadvantaged families. In addition, a comprehensive overview of quality in children's services (Stein, 2009), which provides rigorous reviews of research evidence, exposes the value of positive parenting and the difference this makes to the well-being, welfare and protection of vulnerable children.

Intervention and parenting programmes: developing quality

Evidence exists about the importance of parental collaboration in children's learning (Whalley, 2007; Sarkadi et al., 2008; Digman and Soan, 2008). They tell us that parental partnerships are important for children's welfare, that we should support vulnerable children at an early stage of their lives, and that intervention and support is the key. A range of what we might term parental intervention programmes and intervention projects have been developed, aimed at vulnerable groups who require additional support. Some years ago it could be argued that these might be seen as providing a service which if unchecked might lead to a form of professional dependency, rather than attempt to develop in parents an attitude of self-direction and independence. We are moving away from the 'we know best' model of parental support and intervention, but this in turn means encouraging parents to participate in a form of collaboration or partnership with professionals. Some are 'hard to reach', a description Coe et al. (2008) uses in relation to their work with parents in a multi-cultural community. They found that significant numbers of eligible families were not accessing Sure Start services even though many parents had a positive view of the programme. Other pressures limited their involvement, for example social isolation and difficulty in accessing services, but it was found that contacting parents early and establishing and maintaining positive relationships was important in increasing engagement with families.

There have been extensive studies that consider the quality inter-actions between parents and the types of childcare they access. The Effective Provision of Pre-school Education (EPPE) project (Sylva et al., 2004) carried out a comprehensive study of 3,000 children in early years settings and homes between the ages of three and seven. By the age of three there were already marked differences between individual children's social and intellectual development. It was suggested that an important factor impacting on that difference was the quality of the home learning environment, an effect that continues through to the age of seven. The study concluded that parents who are involved in their children's learning enhance their children's development. But as we have noted, family life is changing – do parents have time to get involved? The *Every Parent Matters* report (DCSF, 2007) considered how practitioners need to respond to the different dynamics of modern-day parenting. Family members may work long hours, and children have many opportunities to keep themselves occupied through television or computer games. Generally, a convenience culture has emerged to enable families to carry out their busy and diverse lives. This may result in less meaningful engagement between parents and children and may require practitioners to provide guidance and sometimes structured intervention strategies to support families in accessing play and learning opportunities. It may also mean offering forms of communication that are based on digital technology especially in terms of providing information and resources as a complement to face-to-face support.

As for parental intervention projects or approaches, there are numerous organisations that have been aimed to develop parental partnerships. The Department for Education in England now holds responsibility for disseminating information from such organisations. One example is the National Academy for Parenting Practitioners (NAPP). Established in 2007 by the DCSF, its aim was to enhance professional skills of those working with parents and families, including training and the delivery of parenting programmes (DCSF, 2009). Other intervention and training projects include the Early Learning Partnership Project (ELPP), which targeted 'hard to reach' and vulnerable parents of children between one and three years of age through a range of approaches. A particular focus was children identified as being at risk of learning delay. The

ELPP was set up in 2006 to test out ways of encouraging parents in disadvantaged families to get involved with their children and their interests. Nine voluntary organisations examined 12 different approaches between October 2006 and March 2008. The evaluation found that the project gave parents new skills, techniques and creative ideas and 'new confidence in their role as educators', but also found that there was little improvement in parenting behaviour that challenged children's thinking or extended their communication skills (Evangelou et al., 2008: ii). The project also focused on ways to improve the skills of the early years workforce, including volunteers, and recognised the value of professional development to build skills of practitioners to support parents. Such intervention requires practitioners to develop what Siraj-Blatchford (2007) sees as supportive yet challenging ways of involving parents and the ability of practitioners to gradually develop more sophisticated communication and collaboration strategies.

The Key Elements of Effective Practice (KEEP) revealed the need for training to improve quality. The project suggested that practitioners need knowledge, the ability to develop a practical response to the needs of parents in the community and the ability to collaborate with other professionals to understand and build on their skills in developing relationships with parents (DfES, 2005). We also have evidence from the Parents Early Years and Learning (PEAL) project, originated in 2007 by a consortium which included the National Children's Bureau (NCB), the Coram family, the London Borough of Camden and the Department for Education and Skills. Its aim was to identify and disseminate existing effective practice in engaging parents, and design and promote training for practitioners and establish links between early years sectors and education. The result was that PEAL supported and trained 1,700 practitioners from approximately 700 children's centres across every government region in 2007/08.

A variety of approaches are being developed by Sure Start Children's Centres in England. These are based on the premise that integrated working makes professionals consider how they can contribute effectively and collectively to support families, rather than expect the family to have the ability to search out and somehow access themselves the services available. This goes some way to enabling children and families to overcome barriers to participation and learning. However, for this to happen it requires efficient leadership and management skills, as it rests on coordinated services providing support, not intrusion within local communities. This can be seen in the *Planning and Performance Management Guidance* for Sure Start centres (DCSF, 2010c), which evaluates the work of centres in the community. The evaluation asks searching questions about aspects of practice. For example, how often are the views of fathers, mothers and others responsible for children gathered? What do these views tell the children's centre about the quality of provision and the appropriateness of services? What mechanisms have been used to engage with and involve families – fathers, mothers and children? These questions are underpinned by values such as recognising the expertise of parents, sharing information, enhancing collaboration and developing the ability to listen. These values can be seen again within the National Quality Improvement Network's *Principles for Engaging with Families*, which advocates developing the skills of the practitioner to find positive ways of working with parents (NQIN, 2010). The project was funded by the Department for Children, Schools and Families to help create and support an early years workforce with the skills, knowledge and the disposition to build respectful relationships with parents of children under three and to help parents to support children's innate readiness to learn. It is hoped that these principles will be used to promote reflection at all levels within children's trusts, local authority teams and settings and improve outcomes for children. The *Principles for Engaging with Families* suggest that successful and sustained engagement with families can be seen when:

- practitioners work alongside families in a valued working relationship;

- practitioners and parents are willing to listen to and learn from each other;

- practitioners respect what families know and already do;

- practitioners find ways to actively engage those who do not traditionally access services;

- parents are seen as decision-makers in organisations and services;

- families' views, opinions and expectations of services are raised and their confidence increases as service users;

- there is support for the whole family;

- there is provision of universal services but with opportunities for more intensive support where most needed;

- there is effective support and supervision for staff, encouraging evaluation and self-reflection;

- there is an honest sharing of issues around safeguarding.

This reinforces similar questions posed by those inspecting early years settings and immediately puts the child at the heart of the process. So what does all this information tell us? Firstly that collaboration with parents and families is important and this is recognised by a range of expert opinion, research evidence and what practitioners themselves say about the value of working in tandem with parents. Collaboration can and does lead to improved opportunities for children's welfare. Realistically, however, there are challenges ahead. To do all this requires time, energy, commitment and the development of many professional skills and dispositions to promote such collaboration. Tenacity, perseverance, reflective thinking, integrity, ethicality and enhanced communication skills are needed, as well as patience and a considerable knowledge of the approaches necessary to work with parents, together with the ability to challenge assumptions and shed preconceived ideas about what the 'ideal family' should look like. It requires what Karen Appleby and Mandy Andrews in Chapter 4 suggest: a necessity to reflect and consider one's own values and beliefs in order to improve quality.

Quality perspectives in practice

When considering examples of how parental partnership and professional support works in practice we should remember that any example is just that: an example. They are only snapshots taken from a much larger photograph album that is the day-to-day practice in the UK. What they represent in terms of quality provision and the enhancement of quality we shall consider after the case studies below. These examples come from the work of practitioners in one local authority, using their 'professional journeys' to illustrate key aspects of how they have worked with parents and for parents in order to improve quality.

Case study 1: Emily's journey

We join Emily's professional journey when she was a supervisor in a small rural pre-school. She worked with the local community in developing a project that focused on ways to improve inclusion for children with additional needs. This was supported by a local authority development team and involved artists based in the setting working alongside children, practitioners and parents. The project was successful, with the results showing that children became actively involved in developing their relationships with others. Emily used her experience from this project when she engaged in Portage Training – a home visiting based programme of parental support that provides planned interventions with parent and child to facilitate the child's development. Importantly, portage work enhances the independence of parents as it provides a supportive framework within which both child and parent can succeed.

Emily's experience in the voluntary (third) sector proved invaluable when she took on a new role working for the local authority at an inner-city children's centre. Here she began work as a family support worker in the community. This involved partnership working with hard-to-reach families. For some it was the first time they had received support from within the community and Emily played a part in encouraging parents to use the services of the children's centre, along with their partners and children. To further increase her experience and knowledge she started a Foundation Degree in Early Years, designed in partnership with the local authority. Tuition took place each week at a local children's centre. This allowed her to practise her skills of evaluation and work-based enquiry, which in turn allowed her to focus on considering inter-agency working in her setting and the way this was meeting the needs of parents. Her support work with families continued and became more specialised, in particular offering support to children with additional needs and sleep difficulties.

Emily now works with parents who have children with sleep problems and she has recently engaged in training as a parental support sleep specialist. She works with all parents as part of her role and acknowledges that every family has different needs. She is gaining more experience as a sleep specialist as sleep issues are common among all children, but more likely to occur among children with additional needs. Researchers estimate that between 40 and 80 per cent of children with additional needs might have problems with sleep (DCSF, 2010b).

Case study 2: Linda's journey

Linda works as a supervisor with young children at a children's centre nursery. A significant influence on her professional views has been Reggio Emilia, ever since she and others visited Italy to explore first hand the 'Reggio approach' to children's learning. Their experience has been long-lasting and alongside other colleagues she has been developing practice that underlines the 'Reggio approach' and a 'values-based approach' that places the child very much at the centre of what goes on in the setting. Learning journeys for all children at whatever age feature highly in this approach and parents play a real and active role in the design and content of these journeys. Indeed, the most recent inspection report for the setting indicated the outstanding partnership between staff and parents. It noted in particular the child-focused approach that was accessible to parents and understood by the local community, and how transitions from home were carefully managed. Linda's nursery provides a window that allows parents to see other services that the children's centre provides, including, for example, family support services, portage, self-help groups and a range of other professionals from health and social services. This underlines the value of professionals working together, because parents rarely look for additional services, but they can be supported and directed towards appropriate services, by listening to their needs and the needs of children.

Linda was not one to neglect her professional development and her story is a success. She first completed a part-time university-based Foundation Degree in Early Years. This was valuable as it allowed her to engage in work-based study and to reflect upon what worked in her practice, what could be improved and where to go next in her professional development. She built upon this experience and moved on to gain Early Years Professional Status, alongside a BA honours degree in Early Childhood Studies. Her focus on improvement remained and centred on leading practice and developing the practice of others. This took some years and a lot of dedication as it was completed while working with children and families. Recent developments in her practice have included the design of an internet-based project that allows parent-to-setting interaction for recording learning. Another has allowed Linda to share her passion for children's education with others and to support new staff in developing ways to support new parents.

These two case studies illustrate how practitioners are changing and developing in terms of providing support for parents and the way they engage in partnership working. They highlight how training and professional development play a strong part in the process and the role of the local authority in encouraging and providing access to training. Last but not least, the case studies reveal the values, tenacity and determination of Emily and Linda to engage with parents. They saw this not just as a professional responsibility but, as Claire Majella Richards suggests in Chapter 8, as the privilege of being invited to 'enter' the world of the parent in order to work collaboratively and support families.

If we return to the *Principles for Engaging with Families* (NQIN, 2010), we can see that both Emily and Linda underpin those principles in their practice. They work alongside families in a valued working relationship. They are non-judgemental and attempt to introduce and encourage parents to take advantage of their knowledge rather than impose their knowledge upon them. In this way practitioners and parents are willing to listen to and learn from each other. They also build on what parents know; in the case of Linda she has built upon the way parents are now adept at using web-based technologies to communicate with each other and indeed with practitioners. Emily considered families needs 'outside the box' and focused on issues that are of powerful concern to them, such as sleep problems (DCSF, 2010b). This allowed her to engage with those who do not traditionally access services as there was a purpose and value to using her expertise.

Both Emily and Linda also see parents as decision-makers within organisations and services, not as the recipients of services. This is not about offering choice, with parents seen as some sort of customer that is 'always right', it is more about developing values within a setting that actually believes that parents have a view and that this should be shared. This is, of course, risky. We are encouraging parents to have a voice, share views and give opinions, especially about their expectations of services. This means that sometimes practitioners are criticised, but for parents it means that their expectations are raised and their confidence increased. Ultimately they may expect more and become less passive about their needs.

As we encourage independence we have to think carefully about a gradual supportive release of professional services to lessen dependency, which also means carefully considering what volume of support is necessary, talking to other agencies, and seeking out and using specialist services. It means looking at the child's needs but also looking at the whole child and their family. All of which sounds wonderful, but with such practice comes the responsibility to listen to one's own values about the importance of partnership with parents, to listen to the research evidence, and to foster independence, not professional dependence.

☐ Summary

Practitioners constantly make moral and logistic decisions about the support they provide to parents. They too need support and supervision and need to be encouraged to engage in evaluation and self-reflection. This may come from the setting itself, but in the case of our two colleagues it was supported and encouraged by their continuing professional development at university. Through their training they were supported in their desire to engage in work-based investigation, to reflect on their own roles and maintain an ongoing dialogue between the course and the setting and develop quality improvement. All this requires dedication, hard work, and a value base that sees parents as the primary educators of their children. It is not easy, but it is important and it will improve quality. Very importantly, it provides a framework that allows an honest sharing of issues around safeguarding, which ultimately will protect the welfare of children. In this way it is important not to see parental partnership as something that is somehow separate or having a place in the 'quality framework' on its own. It is instead an essential and integrated part of improving quality.

References

Athey, C. (1990) *Extending Thought in Young Children: A Parent Teacher Partnership.* London: Paul Chapman.

Baldock, P., Fitzgerald, D. and Kay, J. (2009) *Understanding Early Years Policy* (2nd edition). London: Sage.

Coe, C., Gibson, A., Spencer, N. and Stuttaford, M. (2008) 'Sure Start: voices of the "hard to reach"', *Childcare and Health Development Journal*, 34 (4): 447–53.

Department for Children, Education, Lifelong Learning and Skills (DCELLS) (2008) *Foundation Phase Framework for Children's Learning for 3 to 7 year olds in Wales.* Cardiff: Welsh Assembly Government.

Department for Children, Schools and Families (DCSF) (2007) *Every Parent Matters.* Nottingham: DCSF.

Department for Children, Schools and Families (DCSF) (2008) *Practice Guidance for the Early Years Foundation Stage.* Available at: http://publications.education.gov.uk/eOrderingDownload/eyfs_practiceguid_0026608.pdf (last accessed 2 December 2010).

Department for Children, Schools and Families (DCSF) (2009) *National Academy for Parenting Practitioners.* Available at: http://www.dcsf.gov.uk/everychildmatters/strategy/parents/napp/napp/ (last accessed 15 December 2010).

Department for Children, Schools and Families (DCSF) (2010a) *Breaking the Link Between Disadvantage and Low Achievement in the Early Years.* Nottingham: DCSF.

Department for Children, Schools and Families (DCSF) (2010b) *Information for Parents: Sleep*. Nottingham: DCSF.

Department for Children, Schools and Families (DCSF) (2010c) *Sure Start Children's Centres: Planning and Performance Management Guidance*. Nottingham: DCSF.

Department for Children, Schools and Families (DCSF) (2010d) *Support For All: The Families and Relationships*. Green Paper presented to Parliament by the Secretary of State for Children, Schools and Families, January. London: The Stationery Office.

Department for Education Northern Ireland (DENI), Health, Social Services and Public Safety (2008) *Curricular Guidance for Pre-school Education*. Northern Ireland: Council for the Curriculum, Examinations and Assessment.

Department for Education and Skills (DfES) (2005) *The KEEP project (Key Elements of Effective Practice)*. Nottingham: DCSF. Available at: http://www.niched.org/docs/key%20elements%20of%20effective%20practice%20KEEP.pdf (last accessed 15 December 2010).

Desforges, C. and Abouchaar, A. (2003) *The Impact of Parental Involvement, Parental Support and Family Education on Pupil Achievement and Adjustment: A Literature Review*, Research report RR433. London: DfES.

Digman, C. and Soan, S. (2008) *Working with Parents: A Guide for Educational Professionals*. London: Sage.

Evangelou, M., Sylva, K., Edwards, A. and Smith, T. (2008) *Supporting Parents in Promoting Early Learning*. Nottingham: DCSF and Oxford University.

Gasper, M. (2010) *Multi-agency Working in the Early Years*. London: Sage.

Harris, A., Power, A. and Goodall, J. (2009) *Do Parents Know They Matter? Raising Achievement through Parental Engagement*. London: Continuum.

Hodge, N. and Runswick-Cole, K. (2008) 'Problematising parent-professional partnerships', *Disability & Society*, 23 (6): 637–47.

Jackson, A. (2010) 'Defining and measuring quality in early years settings', in M. Reed and N. Canning (eds), *Reflective Practice in the Early Years*. London: Sage.

Kidner, C. (2010) *SPICe Briefing: Curriculum for Excellence 02/10*. Edinburgh: Scottish Parliament. Available at: http://www.scottish.parliament.uk/business/research/briefings-10/SB10-10.pdf (last accessed 15 December 2010).

Leading Parent Partnership Award (LPPA) (2010) *For Schools and Settings Committed to Investing in Parents and Carers for the Achievement of Pupils and Students*. Available at: http://www.lppa.co.uk (last accessed 15 December 2010).

Maplethorpe, N., Chanfreau, J., Philo, D. and Tait, C. (2010) *Families with Children in Britain: Findings from the 2008 Families and Children Study (FACS)*. London: DWP and the National Centre for Social Research.

Meade, A. (1995) *Thinking Children and Learning about Schemas*. New Zealand: NZCER Press.

Moss, P., Brophy, J. and Stratham, J. (2007) 'Parental involvement in playgroups', *Children in Society*, 6 (4): 297–316.

National Quality Improvement Network (NQIN) (2007) *Quality Improvement Principles: A Framework for Local Authorities and National Organisations to Improve Quality Outcomes for Children and Young People*. London: National Children's Bureau.

National Quality Improvement Network (NQIN) (2010) *Principles for Engaging with Families*. London: National Children's Bureau.

Reed, M. and Walker, R. (2010) 'Parental partnerships', in N. Canning (ed.), *Play and Practice in the Early Years Foundation Stage*. London: Sage.

Rhodes, H. (2008) 'Love matters – Family and Parenting Institute', conference paper, Nottingham Early Intervention International Conference. Available at: http://www.nottinghamcity.gov.uk/CHttpHandler.ashx?id=8860&p=0 (last accessed 15 December 2010).

Sarkadi, A., Kristansson, R., Oberklaid, F. and Brembergs, S. (2008) 'Fathers' involvement and children's development outcomes: a systematic review of longitudinal studies', *Acta Paediatrica Nurturing the Child*, 97 (2): 153–8.

Scottish Government (2008) *Curriculum for Excellence: Building the Curriculum 3: A Framework for Learning and Teaching.* Edinburgh: Scottish Government. Available at: http://www.ltscotland.org.uk/Images/building_the_curriculum_3_jms3_tcm4-489454.pdf (last accessed 15 December 2010).

Siraj-Blatchford, I. (2007) 'Creativity, communication and collaboration: the identification of pedagogic progression in sustained shared thinking', *Asia-Pacific Journal of Research in Early Childhood Education*, 1 (2): 3–24.

Stein, M. (2009) *Quality Matters in Children's Services: Messages from Research.* London and Philadelphia: Jessica Kingsley.

Sylva, K., Melhuish, E., Sammons, P., Siraj-Blatchford, I. and Taggart, B. (2004) *The Effective Provision of Pre-school Education (EPPE) Project: Findings from Pre-school to end of Key Stage 1.* London: DfES.

Whalley, M. (2007) *Involving Parents in their Children's Learning* (2nd edition). London: Sage.

Wheeler, H., Connor, J. and Goodwin, H. (2009) *Parents, Early Years and Learning: Parents as Partners in the Early Years Foundation Stage: Principles into Practice.* London: National Children's Bureau.

11

Improving quality in the early years: starting with the student experience

Carla Solvason

Chapter overview

This chapter, written about practitioners for practitioners, considers the roles, responsibilities and relationships that have been developed through working with a local authority in order to enhance early childhood student experiences. It asks questions about the ways in which we approach professional collaboration and share professional expertise within the context of supporting Foundation Degree students during their work-based learning. It explores a partnership that was created around the student, which aimed to cater for the complex needs of the developing early years practitioner, and by doing so, ultimately to improve the quality of experiences for young children in our care. My role within this was a participant observer, and an ethical approach was taken to record this process, which I shall discuss fully in this chapter.

Foundation Degrees are sometimes viewed as the poor relation to other more 'academic' degrees, but only by those who are unaware of how fundamental this qualification is as a route to improving quality within the early years sector. It was with a clear vision of its importance that two colleagues and myself took on the responsibility of managing a partnership working with eight colleges that delivered our Foundation Degree in Early Years. This degree is work or practice based; it requires students to carry out development tasks within their own workplace or agreed setting while they also attend taught modules, usually for one day per week. One of our priorities was to restructure our approach to supporting students within their workplace. Our vision was to model the type of inter-agency working that featured so highly in *Every Child Matters* (ECM) (DfES, 2004a) and to work collaboratively with others in order to fulfil the needs of both our students and, more long term, young children within settings.

Every Child Matters was a seminal policy that completely changed the way that early years childcare is viewed. Rather than distinct pockets of support, representing health, social care and educational systems, between which children could easily slip, ECM proposed that these services work together within a fully integrated system. By streamlining communication with families through multi-disciplinary teams based in schools and children's centres, it was hoped that problems could be recognised, and intervention put in place, much earlier than previously. The safeguarding of children was central to this policy. Although no one approach is perfect, the benefits of an integrated system far outweigh the complications. The *Five Year Strategy for Children and Learners* (DfES, 2004b: 20) sums up the spirit of collaborative working in the sentence: 'Children do not distinguish their needs based on which agencies run which services – neither should we.'

Building the team around the student

Since the introduction of this multi-disciplinary approach, a range of terminology has emerged, including partnership, multi-agency, collaborative, inter-professional and integrated services. Although some theorists have offered differing definitions and analyses of these terms (Lloyd et al., 2001), in order to clarify the murky waters that it is claimed so many synonyms has created (Anning et al., 2006; Brown and White, 2006), I would argue that such definitions are both spurious and pedantic. All the terms, simply mean to share differing skills and understandings to work together towards the best outcome for children and families. As such most of these terms are appropriate. Although the DfES (2004a) inter-agency approach was originally designed primarily to safeguard vulnerable children and young people, it inadvertently opened our eyes to a whole new way of working and thinking. ECM made clear that no one professional was expected to know all the answers, because each was no more than a cog in a much larger and more complex machine. Each cog was small, but vital if the machine was to keep functioning. At the same time as acknowledging the limitations of each individual's knowledge and skills, it also recognised how vital it was that each one of those cogs performed their own job correctly; if this did not happen, then the whole engine would break down. Each and every one of us became equally accountable for the children with whom we came into contact.

By recognising the limitations of our own experience and current skills base as university tutors, we saw the value in drawing upon knowledge and expertise of Early Years local authority (LA) advisors, who had a sound knowledge and understanding of settings within which our students were based. With a shared vision for improving the quality of experiences for young children, these advisors agreed to support our students within their work-based learning. This began our own process of developing an inter-agency *team around the student*. This team aimed to cater for the many facets of the student's experience, by providing support for their studies through academic tutors, support for their well-being through personal tutors, but also acknowledging them as professionals in the workplace. As such we believed that the supervision that students received within the workplace should be quite different from other student/tutor relationships, and that the practising professional should be able to opt in or out of it as they saw fit. For this consultancy role we felt that LA advisors were ideal as they had a true picture of both settings and students' needs.

Our reasons for reassessing this role were primarily because 'setting support' would sometimes take the form of proofreading assignments and 'ticking off' files. In the past all the early years students' work-based learning had been overseen by a college-based appointed tutor, who sometimes took on the role of 'agony aunt' listening to the student's difficulties in coping with their study requirements. This made the whole process rather insular and focused on academic outcomes rather than on real practice and setting improvements. However much the college tutor's knowledge of the setting grew with familiarity, the input that students received was limited to one knowledge base, which was that of the Foundation Degree community. Engeström (2001) comments that we need to see learning horizontally, rather than vertically, and avoid always attempting to elevate ourselves upward. We needed to prevent a narrow focus on academic success and instead look at the knowledge to be gained from those around us. I would add to Engeström's comment that a vital part of horizontal 'learning' is not the simple acquisition of knowledge from others, but a greater understanding of how we can create and best utilise alliances with others. We feel that we have taken great strides in this area with our team around the student.

Although all educators know the value of the 'learning journey', it is only natural for the focus sometimes to become skewed to more summative indicators of success, and the 'assessed task' has often become the focus of setting visits by tutors or mentors. By attempting to leave that area to academic tutors, the LA advisors would be able to concentrate on the fundamental aim of the course – improving the quality of care and educational experiences for children. In a slight tangent to the 'team around the child' (a term coined by Siraj-Blatchford in 2007 in the avalanche of literature espousing inter-agency working), we envisaged the student gaining from the expertise of both the LA advisor and college tutor. Through this we hoped to cater for many more of the complexities of the student's learning experience. Just as in our current climate of safeguarding children responsibility is shared by all, so we aimed to create a quality support system of multiple roles, but with a shared responsibility for the student.

Within this system there would be clearly defined roles, but no enduring dominant role. The academic tutors focused on college work, and LA advisors on carrying out tasks within settings. Within this new system university and college tutors and LA advisors have an overlapping duty of care for the student, but they also have very clearly defined and very different responsibilities. Engeström (2001: 147) refers to such an approach as 'knotworking', where different services come to work closely together on realising that they share a 'mutually monitored long-term plan'. This is quite different from the interpretation of knotworking by Atkinson et al. (2007), which suggests a more fleeting alliance of convenience.

Wenger and Snyder (2000) describe communities of practice as a group of people meeting regularly in order to learn how to do something better. The community of practice that we created came together in an attempt to improve the calibre of the professional within early years settings and as a result to improve quality within settings. As university tutors we recognised that we were not those with first-hand knowledge of the needs of the settings in which Foundation

Degree students were developing their skills, but those supporting settings through the local authority were. Therefore our community of practice is somewhat unique, in that although we share a passion and a vision, unlike Wenger's model we do not share a profession. With a mutual respect for our differing areas of expertise, academic tutors have created an allegiance with early years LA advisors in order to offer the best possible support for our students. Although the immediate aim is to produce a high-calibre early years professional, the long-term goal, shared with the local authority, is to improve quality in all early years settings.

On the whole, people do not tend to take warmly to change; it brings with it the fear of the unknown and can upset equilibriums. The reconceptualisation and acceptance of new systems is easier for some than for others (Bandura, 1997). So it would have been naive to expect that any such reimagining (Tormey and Henchy, 2008) of an approach to teaching the Foundation Degree could happen seamlessly, or that our belief in the worthiness of such an approach would necessarily mean that it was adopted by all without reluctance. This chapter presents a brief overview, tracing the creation of a new learning community from its inception to its established functioning. It looks at the shuffling that needed to take place when two quite diverse and established working groups began to work together and how doubts and anxieties gradually became shared enthusiasms, driven by the shared vision of improving the quality of the care and learning experience for young children. In creating a new system we caused 'disturbances and conflicts, but also innovative attempts to change the activity' (Engeström, 2001: 137). Such innovation Engeström describes as the 'third space'. When a new collaboration is formed a new window of opportunity is opened up and horizons are widened.

An overview of the research process

The views of LA advisors and Foundation Degree students were vital within the development of the degree and the process would have been pointless if we had not considered their voices. The aim was to research 'with' the students and LA advisors, as participant observers, as opposed to researching 'on' them (James, 2004). The research explores the restructuring of a community of practice, and attempts to present experiences from a number of perspectives and to give a voice to all of those involved in various roles. At this point the research is focused on the 'detailed workings of the relationships and social processes, rather than . . . the outcomes of these' (Denscombe, 2007: 36). It was very shortly after the inception of this collaboration that it was decided that it would be a good idea to record it for research purposes. For this reason all participants in both the Partnership and Mentor forums were asked whether they had any objection to comments being recorded and potentially used for research purposes. In addition it was agreed that any literature to be published in the public domain would first be verified by all partners who had been a party to the discussion or involved in activities.

As a work in progress, at the time of writing (2011) we are delighted by the effect that this partnership has had so far. It is an ongoing development that is by no means completed and one that may take another year to complete a first cycle. It takes an 'Action research' approach, in that the 'driving force . . . [is] . . . an impetus for change/innovation' (Noffke and Somekh, 2005: 91). Greenbank (2007: 99) discusses how 'the reiterative action research cycle of planning, action, evaluation and reflection is a process that teachers in higher education intuitively adopt'. I would stress that this is not something specific to higher education but applies to the reflective practitioner in general, and a premise on which I attempt to make research more tangible to my early years students. As practitioners we are constantly 'trying things out' and measuring the effects. The distinction is that in recognising something as a piece of academic research and something worthy of dissemination, we formalise the process and attempt to make it more rigorous. Fortunately for all involved, this collaborative development was not introduced to the community as a piece of research and was not intended as such. This would most certainly have disturbed the 'power differentials', as discussed by Greenbank (2007: 101). A partner in a development is a very different role from that of a participant in research. This was not introduced as a piece of research, as our sole intention at the outset was to use the expertise of others to improve student practice. Only later did we realise how innovative the approach had proved and the necessity for systematically recording the process.

As is often the case with any qualitative investigation, this research was adopted and modified as the study progressed 'because of the social realities of doing research among and within the living' (Janesick, 1994: 218). Broadly, however, the developments under investigation can be grouped within five phases (see Table 11.1).

Table 11.1 The research process

Research phase	Actions taken
Phase One	New partnership team recognised the need to work more closely with local authorities in empowering students as autonomous professionals.
Phase Two	Agreement gained from the workforce development lead that they would deliver the 'mentor' role within the newly established Foundation Degree in Early Years.
Phase Three	Introduction of this proposal to the team of early years LA advisors, asking them to pilot the initiative. The early years team immediately adopted and began to develop this role. It is here that we asked for permission and began to record data.
Phase Four	Early years LA advisors began to carry out the mentor role, and in doing so developed facets of it. Their views formed the basis of literature supporting the role. The LA advisors met regularly with university staff to monitor the progress of students and air any problems.
Phase Five	End of first year review.

What follows is a short narrative of some of my experiences as a university tutor, but through notes taken at meetings and through semi-structured interviews I will also attempt to present the views of other participants in a lengthier project report to be completed in the future. It is important to at least attempt to obtain a view of how 'the people being studied see their world' (Denscombe, 2007: 62), though in reality this proves problematic. Although this investigation explores just one aspect of the research it most definitely has wider implications for other work-based degrees (Denscombe, 2007).

Early findings

The first physical meetings (which Engeström, 2001 refers to as boundary crossing) for this collaboration were difficult due to the need to shift concepts and re-establish roles within this newly formed community. There was the need for both parties (university and LA advisors) to understand the 'who we are and what we do' about the other in order to establish trust (Broadhead and Armistead, 2007). Despite the enthusiasms of university staff and the LA Workforce Development Lead, the first meeting with early years LA advisors was somewhat overshadowed by the many concerns that a changed role would bring. The LA advisors were clearly apprehensive about the new system, in terms of both their limited understanding of academic systems and their limited time. It was not until the next meeting that we could begin to find some common ground, and there was a tentative feeling that the two factions may indeed 'face similar problems, share a passion for the same topics . . . and approaches' where they could contribute (Wenger et al., 2002: 71). It was only in later meetings that we could really begin to spend time exploring 'what . . . [we] could build on and imagining where this potential could lead' (Wenger et al., 2002: 72). As Engeström (2001) describes, those initial disturbances created open ground for new innovations.

The concept of this collaboration was then aired at a Partnership Forum, a wide-reaching meeting involving LA representatives from a number of authorities, course leaders from those authorities and academic tutors. During this meeting a 'shared vision' was drafted. Within this discussion the importance of Thought Leaders, 'well seasoned and well respected practitioners', became apparent (Wenger et al., 2002: 78). As a group of academics detached from 'reality', our ideas would have lacked resonance, but backed by articulate and visionary LA leaders they became tangible. Although there were immediate concerns raised concerning the impact on LA advisors' time, most of the comments (see Figure 11.1) positively viewed the longitudinal impact of the new collaboration and its potential impact on settings.

During this first Partnership Forum meeting there was surprisingly little resistance to the concept of greater involvement from the local authorities. It was as the role was 'fleshed out' with the advisors that more unexpected barriers emerged. These planning meetings involved the LA advisors who would be taking on the 'mentor' role, their manager and university and college tutors. During the second meeting deadlock was reached over the new title that the 'mentors' should have. This became vitally important to the LA advisors in the creation of their new identity. It actually took two meetings during which words like professional, partner, quality, support, facilitator,

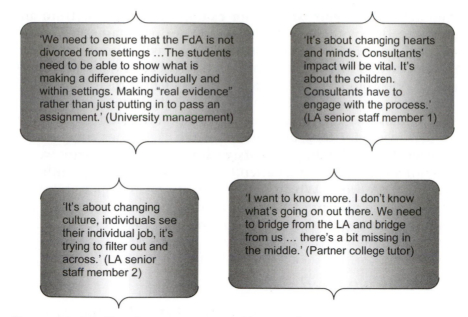

Figure 11.1 Reflections on a new collaboration

improvement, guide, coach, advisor and others were all considered. Although 'Quality Consultant' was used in the early stages, it was finally agreed that 'Professional Practice Consultant' (PPC) encompassed the role that they envisioned themselves becoming. Here Bandura's (1997) reconceptualisation was clearly demonstrated.

The LA advisors had their own wealth of knowledge, understanding and skills, but needed guidance to assimilate these within the degree qualification environment. Within the community that was formed there needed to be a co-construction of new identities (Somekh and Lewin, 2005) and as the university tutors stepped back the LA advisors stepped forward. Over the first two meetings it was interesting to see the LA advisors change from passive respondents into assertive partners in the creation of their role and their potential for contribution. Channels for communication and mutual understanding had opened up and as such the community became a site of innovation (Seaman, 2008: 272). Wenger (1998: 82) comments: 'Over time, the joint pursuit of an enterprise creates resources for negotiating meaning', and such has been the case throughout the partnership so far. The LA advisor's increasing contact with and understanding of the Foundation Degree has enabled them to vocalise their own perspectives of the requirements of their role and the needs of the student.

There have been some barriers, for example between the third and fourth meetings with the Professional Practice Consultants (PPC); when they had gained more 'hands-on experience' with the students they had slipped into that classic 'agony aunt' role. They expressed concern that no one would be 'looking after' the student if their relationship were purely professional. They were reassured of the many different professionals that comprised the 'team around the student', and that the personal tutor took on a pastoral role. A further complication has been that in linking students with their local authority we are left with some students that attend training outside of the authority in which they work. Which local authority takes responsibility for supporting the student? Although inroads have been made with this it is still under negotiation and development.

Where are we now?

Since their inception PPC review meetings have taken place regularly (with notes recorded) and the role is still being developed. The PPC is now a pivotal role in the newly revalidated degree and is clearly outlined in course handbooks. At a recent evening for prospective students at a pilot college, collaboratively hosted by university, college and local authorities, the local authorities Workforce Development Lead took on the responsibility (with no prompting from the university) of introducing the PPC role to the new students. This she

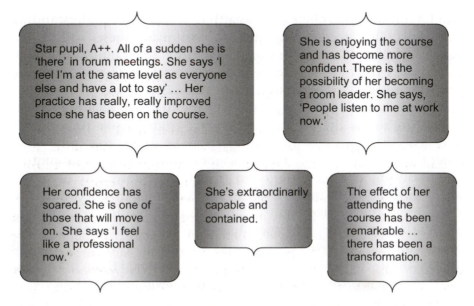

Figure 11.2 Professional practice consultants' reflections

saw as part of her team's responsibility and marked a seminal point in the development of this role as its 'ownership' shifted to the local authority staff. Even more exciting was the final update meeting of the academic year, between LA advisors, college and university tutors. The comments made about the students demonstrated perfectly the type of growth and development in the students that we had envisaged this partnership bringing about. Figure 11.2 presents some of the comments made by the Professional Practice Consultants about the students within their care.

What really came through from the comments was the empowerment of the students. Although many had received support some simply felt that they did not need it, and although their situation was monitored advice was not forced upon them.

☐ Summary

Although dealing with cuts within the advisory service our pilot PPCs were extremely positive about taking on an additional cohort of students and were eager for us to reach the numbers required for us to roll out the programme for a second year. Discussions are currently under way with other local authorities in the hope that they, too, will become partners in this scheme. Discussion groups are planned with the pilot students in order to obtain their views on the success or otherwise of this venture. What has worked well for them, and how do they see the role developing? It would seem that in lessening the professional distance between ourselves (academic tutors) and the local authority we have also lessened the distance, at least in some cases, between practitioners and advisors. Our shared vision to improve quality in settings appears to be having an impact and we will continue to monitor the development of this new community of practice.

References

Anning, A., Cottrell, D., Frost, N., Green, J. and Robinson, M. (2006) *Developing Multi-professional Teamwork for Integrated Children's Services*. London: McGraw-Hill.

Atkinson, M., Lamont, E. and Jones, M. (2007) *Multiagency Working and its Implication for Practice: A Review of the Literature*. Reading: CfBT Education Trust.

Bandura, A. (1997) 'Self-efficacy', *Harvard Mental Health Letter*, 13 (9): 4–7.

Broadhead, P. and Armistead, J. (2007) 'Community partnerships: integrating early education with childcare', *Children and Society*, 21 (1): 42–55.

Brown, K. and White, K. (2006) *Exploring the Evidence Base for Integrated Children's Services*. Edinburgh: Scottish Executive Education Department.

Denscombe, M. (2007) *The Good Research Guide for Small-Scale Social Research Projects*. Maidenhead: Open University Press.

Department for Education and Skills (DfES) (2004a) *Every Child Matters: Change for Children*. Nottingham: DfES.

Department for Education and Skills: (DfES) (2004b) *Five Year Strategy for Children and Learners*. London: The Stationery Office.

Engeström, Y. (2001) 'Expansive learning at work: toward an activity theoretical conceptualisation', *Journal of Education and Work*, 14 (1): 133–56.

Greenbank, P. (2007) 'Utilising collaborative forms of educational action research: some reflections', *Journal of Further and Higher Education*, 31 (2): 97–108.

James, D. (2004) *Research in Practice: Experiences, Insights and Interventions*. London: LSDA.

Janesick, V.J. (1994) 'The dance of qualitative research design', in N.K. Denzin (ed.), *Handbook of Qualitative Research*. California: Sage.

Lloyd, G., Stead, J. and Kendrick, A. (2001) *Hanging On in There: A Study of Inter-agency Work to Prevent School Exclusion in Three Local Authorities*. London: National Children's Bureau.

Noffke, S. and Somekh, B. (2005) *Action Research*. London: Sage.

Seaman, M. (2008) 'Birds of a feather? Communities of practice and knowledge communities', *Curriculum and Teaching Dialogue*, 10 (1&2): 269–79.

Siraj-Blatchford, I., Clarke, K. and Needham, M. (2007) *The Team Around the Child: Multi-agency Working in the Early Years*. Stoke-on-Trent: Trentham Books.

Somekh, B. and Lewin, C. (2005) *Research Methods in the Social Sciences*. London: Sage.

Tormey, R. and Henchy, D. (2008) 'Re-imagining the traditional lecture: an action research approach to teaching student teachers to "do" philosophy', *Teaching in Higher Education*, 13 (3): 303–14.

Wenger, E. (1998) *Communities of Practice: Learning, Meaning and Identity*. New York: Cambridge University Press.

Wenger, E. and Snyder, W. (2000) 'Communities of practice: the organizational frontier', *Harvard Business Review*, 78 (1): 139–45.

Wenger, E., McDermott, R. and Snyder, W.M. (2002) *Cultivating Communities of Practice*. Boston, MA: Harvard Business School Press.

Conclusion

Michael Reed and Natalie Canning

Quality can be seen in a microcosm where the impact of change and improvement is seen as localised and specific to a setting or community. However, in this book we have argued that perceptions of quality have to be located within a wider social, cultural and political context which considers issues such as the role of leadership, power relationships and the influence of outside agencies. The wider implications for quality are constantly changing through political and social influences and are further refined by the economic well-being of the country. This allows us to consider the process and experiences that children engage in. We have placed these at the centre of the argument that quality practice and change is an essential component of early years. The book has attempted to do this through exploring a diverse range of subjects in each of the chapters. It has also revealed the perceptions of practitioners and how they celebrate what works, how they analyse what does not and how they consider what can be built on to improve quality experiences. Many of the contributors have discussed the importance of personal reflection on practice and the way in which practitioners can influence a child's environment. We have therefore identified a strand that runs through the book: quality improvement emerges from recognising the impact of a practitioner's decisions and actions and how they can *support* but can also *detract* from children's experiences. Therefore, the book has attempted to challenge, question, refine, develop, change, review, shape and shed preconceived ideas of quality.

Throughout the book quality is exposed in the individual ways practitioners work and approach quality improvement and change. Many of the chapters have argued for practitioners to have ownership and be inside their own practice. Being able to reflect on individual preferences and strengths and where there are areas for development has been identified in each section of the book. Another key theme is the careful examination of individual values and beliefs. Knowing what these are and how they emerge through practice is an important element of engaging in quality improvement because values and beliefs shape practice and are reflected in what practitioners say and do. We have argued that in the debate surrounding quality, values and beliefs lead the way in striving for quality improvement and change within an early years context.

The question, 'What is quality?' has been addressed in each of the sections of the book. If we are honest, it remains unanswered, or perhaps more suitably, 'difficult to define'. However, through analysing quality and change perhaps we are closer to a coherent understanding of what forms the main components of quality practice in the early years. This certainly involves a process of self-reflection, which in itself is important but even more so when coupled with actions and a clear rationale, knowledge and understanding that quality emerges from everyday practice. The book has also been about professional development and the importance of challenging the view of quality as solely developing mechanistic competencies and skills. Instead we have argued that quality improvement needs to be seen as a process focusing on considered knowledge that allows an understanding of what needs to be done and why. It has been important to recognise the motivation of practitioners, the leadership within a setting, the inherent goodwill and the dedication of those who want to see children do well. Another important aspect of the book has been to highlight the need for all children to have access to quality, through analysing not only what happens in practice but also the impact of external influences on the early years sector. External influences can be about regulation, but rarely does regulation in itself promote quality, although it may claim to measure it. Therefore, many of the chapters have argued that quality is a complicated mix of interrelated aspects of practice and that the judgements practitioners make are central to the way in which quality improvement in early years practice continues to evolve.

Ensuring that children remain at the heart of practice enables the debate surrounding quality improvement and change to remain 'on track'. Children's experiences are reflected not only in the quality of practice but in the knowledge and understanding that underpins practice and wider decisions that affect children's lives. The way in which decisions are made has been identified as central to how quality and change emerge from existing practice. Consequently, the book has recognised the significance of research and policy in practice. We have argued that continuing practice which champions quality requires a questioning response to what happens on a day-to-day basis. It requires personal and professional reflection on what has gone before, an understanding of current practice and planning for the future and how improvements to practice and proactive change can result in positive differences for children and families.

Index

Added to a page number 'f' denotes a figure and 't' denotes a table.